BLESSED ARE THEY

True Stories of God's Love in Action

Compiled and Edited by
Céleste Perrino-Walker

Pacific Press® Publishing Association
Nampa, Idaho | www.pacificpress.com

Cover resources from the author
Cover and interior photographs from Versacare
Inside design by Aaron Troia

Copyright © 2019 by Pacific Press® Publishing Association
Printed in the United States of America
All rights reserved

The authors assume full responsibility for the accuracy of all facts and quotations as cited in this book.

Scripture quotations marked NIV® are from THE HOLY BIBLE, NEW INTERNATIONAL VERSION®. Copyright © 1973, 1978, 1984, 2011 by Biblica, Inc.® Used by permission. All rights reserved worldwide.

Scripture marked NKJV is taken from the New King James Version®. Copyright © 1982 by Thomas Nelson. Used by permission. All rights reserved.

Additional copies of this book may be purchased by calling toll-free 1-800-765-6955 or by visiting AdventistBookCenter.com.

Library of Congress Cataloging-in-Publication Data
Names: Walker, Celeste Perrino, compiler.
Title: Blessed are they / compiled and edited by Celeste Perrino-Walker.
Description: Nampa : Pacific Press Publishing Association, 2018. | Includes bibliographical
    references and index.
Identifiers: LCCN 2018052517 | ISBN 9780816364664 (pbk. : alk. paper)
Subjects: LCSH: Adventists—Biography.
Classification: LCC BX6191 .B54 2018 | DDC 286.7092/2 [B] —dc23 LC record available at
    https://lccn.loc.gov/2018052517

February 2019

Now when Jesus saw the crowds, he went up on a mountainside and sat down. His disciples came to him, and he began to teach them.

He said:

> *"Blessed are the poor in spirit,*
>   *for theirs is the kingdom of heaven.*
> *Blessed are those who mourn,*
>   *for they will be comforted.*
> *Blessed are the meek,*
>   *for they will inherit the earth.*
> *Blessed are those who hunger and thirst for righteousness,*
>   *for they will be filled.*
> *Blessed are the merciful,*
>   *for they will be shown mercy.*
> *Blessed are the pure in heart,*
>   *for they will see God.*
> *Blessed are the peacemakers,*
>   *for they will be called children of God.*
> *Blessed are those who are persecuted because of righteousness,*
>   *for theirs is the kingdom of heaven."*

—Matthew 5:1–12, NIV

Contents

Foreword	9
Preface	11
Introduction	13
"Blessed are the poor in spirit, . . ."	**15**
Bring-Your-Sibling-to-School Day: Amistad International	16
The Brightest Light: La Sierra University Enactus	19
Unintended Consequences: La Sierra University Center for Near Eastern Archaeology	22
The Making of a Lady: Youth and Family Life Education Institute	25
The Next Step: Camp Ida-Haven	28
Sewing and Growing: Amistad International	31
"Blessed are those who mourn, . . ."	**35**
An End and a Beginning: Project Patch	36
The Worst of Times: The Unforgettables Foundation	39
Back From Broken: Thunderbird Adventist Academy	42
Little Girl Lost: Adventist Health International	45
The Unexpected: The Unforgettables Foundation	48
"Blessed are the meek, . . ."	**51**
The Nick of Time: Project Patch	52
Breaking the Cycle: Holbrook Indian School	55
Just the Beginning: La Sierra University Center for Near Eastern Archaeology	58
The Ripple Effect: Zoz Amba Foundation	61
Courageous Compassion: Holbrook Indian School	64
"Blessed are those who hunger and thirst for righteousness, . . ."	**67**
Go Healthy for Good: Hope Channel	68
Call to Action: Good News TV	71

New Challenges, New Opportunities: 74
   Cuba Adventist Theological Seminary
Sola Scriptura: Good News TV 76
Miracle Water: Pine Springs Ranch 79
Radio's Long Reach: Your Story Hour 82

"Blessed are the merciful, . . ." **85**
Parenting 2.0: Helping Hands Caregiver Resource Center 86
Settling Old Scores: International Children's Care 89
The Witch of Barillal: Water for Life International 92
Doctor, Come Quickly! Scheer Memorial Adventist Hospital 95
Answering the Call: International Children's Care 98
Delivered From Desperation: Helping Hands 101
   Caregiver Resource Center

"Blessed are the pure in heart, . . ." **105**
Buried Alive: Scheer Memorial Adventist Hospital 106
Hunt for Success: Mamawi Atosketan Native School 109
Truck Exchange: Water for Life International 112
The Best Gift: Zoz Amba Foundation 114
Rounds and Around: Adventist Health International 117

"Blessed are the peacemakers, . . ." **121**
A Better Way: The Center for Conflict Resolution 122
   at La Sierra University
Hope's Mission: Mamawi Atosketan Native School 126
Grandma "Jonah": ASAP Ministries 129
Move Over, Mountain: Youth and Family Life Education Institute 132
The Peaceful Path: The Center for Conflict Resolution 135
   at La Sierra University

"Blessed are those who are persecuted because of righteousness, . . ." **139**
Unshakable: Cuba Adventist Theological Seminary 140
Trial by Fire: Pine Springs Ranch 143
The Tug of Truth: Hope Channel 146
Traffic Stop: Washington Adventist University Enactus 149
Rescued: ASAP Ministries 152

Ministries	**155**
Adventist Health International	156
Amistad International	156
ASAP Ministries	157
Camp Ida-Haven	158
The Center for Conflict Resolution at La Sierra University	159
Cuba Adventist Theological Seminary	160
Enactus	161
Good News TV	162
Helping Hands Caregiver Resource Center	163
Holbrook Indian School	164
Hope Channel	165
La Sierra University Center for Near Eastern Archaeology	166
Mamawi Atosketan Native School	167
Pine Springs Ranch	168
Project Patch	169
Scheer Memorial Adventist Hospital	170
Thunderbird Adventist Academy	171
Your Story Hour	173
Youth and Family Life Education Institute	174
Zoz Amba Foundation	175

Foreword

This book is a real and practical demonstration of the power of God linked with our willingness to help others. It shows the blessings of ministry—blessings for those being ministered to and those doing the ministering. And best of all, we get to be the ministers!

When I became involved in ministry with my family through International Children's Care (ICC) back in 1984, I thought the great blessing of ministry was watching God provide opportunities to people, especially those who seemed to have the worst lot in life.

It was true. I marveled at the lives changed, the communities becoming healthier, and people finding a saving relationship with Jesus through the ministry of ICC. Essentially, I realized I was helping to provide opportunities. Kids who lost their mommy could get a new mommy. A child who wasn't going to school anymore could go to school again. A young person who had no hope of a college education or vocational training had a chance to be prepared for a productive and fulfilling life. Best of all, we saw each soul we touched having the opportunity to connect with Jesus and feel the joy of the hope of eternal life.

But when I thanked the donors who sacrificed to make this all possible and let them know how grateful the kids are for another chance in life, for food, for clothing, for the education they never thought possible, and for a hope that endures forever, the donor would have a most surprising reaction.

"No!" they would exclaim. "I need to thank *you*. My joy is in the blessing I received from God when I took the opportunity to give."

I saw that Jesus really is in the business of providing opportunities: opportunities to the children touched by ministry, opportunities to those who are moved by the Holy Spirit to give, and opportunities for an enduring hope.

But I had another lesson to learn about God's blessings in ministry.

It seems that all ministries face financial challenges—ups and downs—good times and not-so-good times. During one of those difficult times, my wife Sharon and I were visiting the ICC children's village in the Dominican Republic. I woke in the morning a bit late, in a different time zone, to the warm tones of voices singing about the love of God. I walked to the campus office near our guest room and found the staff gathered, as they do every morning, singing and praising God, preparing for another day. They weren't complaining to God about what they lacked. They were thanking God for providing, and they declared their trust in His care. I could feel God's presence in that office.

A little later I visited the farm and found the fathers and older boys gathering to begin their day taking care of the crops and animals. They, too, were singing and praising God, asking Him to guide them through their day. They weren't complaining that their paycheck was a little late or that the food on the table was a bit plain. I could feel God speaking to me in that field.

That evening the whole campus gathered to worship together, and I heard the children singing and praising God. They loved God with newfound, simple, childish faith. They were thankful for what they had. I could hear God whispering to my heart in that church.

Now who was receiving the blessing? I knew it was not only the children who were the object of ministry, and not only the people who gave sacrificially to help the ministry, but that God was blessing *me* deeply, filling *me* with joy, strengthening *my* faith, and renewing *my* determination to walk humbly with my God. I felt Him speaking to my heart. Yes, I, too, was blessed by this ministry.

Versacare has served for many years as a catalyst for ministry, a group of the faithful humbly asking God to use the funds that are entrusted to them for good, for opportunities, for blessing. This book is a wonderful collection of stories and pictures demonstrating these things. I have witnessed the powerful impact Versacare has made by seeing many projects firsthand. In partnership with International Children's Care, Versacare has benefited and blessed countless orphaned children through the years.

With all the competing needs from so many voices asking for funds, how can you feel good about giving to ministry? Where should your funds go? Versacare has developed clear standards of trust with many Adventist organizations, and its partnerships are strengthened by high standards of reporting and accountability. Although Versacare does not recommend one charity over another, it hopes that this book and their website can serve to inspire and guide as you think about how you want to be involved in ministry.

As you read through these stories, they will *introduce* you to ministry, *instruct* you in ministry, *instill* you with confidence in ministry, and certainly you can't help but be *inspired* to minister. Because the best thing of all is that *you* are the minister!

—Rick Fleck,
president of International Children's Care

Preface

For Christians, there is no such thing as coincidence; instead, there are divine appointments. In the fall of 2017, I had a divine appointment with blessing. Shortly after I began collecting the stories you are about to read, I experienced heartache and loss when I walked through the valley of the shadow of divorce. Every day as I collected, compiled, and edited these stories, God blessed me again and again by showing me what He can do through us when we are completely surrendered to Him. Each story demonstrates how He blesses the world through us and proves how, in giving, we are not depleted. Instead, we also receive a blessing.

It's tempting to think "blessing" equals happiness, but it doesn't. If we are blessed, we will not automatically be happy. We will be *more* than happy. Disasters, problems, conflict, and difficult people can all rob us of happiness, but no power on earth can steal God's blessing. Happiness is a fleeting emotion, whereas blessing is the deep contentment of following God no matter what the situation, no matter what the obstacles to overcome, no matter what the conflict, *no matter what*.

The famous preacher Charles Spurgeon said, "If none of God's saints were poor and tried, we should not know half so well the consolations of divine grace. When we find the wanderer who has nowhere to lay his head, who yet can say, 'Still will I trust in the Lord;' when we see the pauper starving on bread and water, who still glories in Jesus; when we see the bereaved widow overwhelmed in affliction, and yet having faith in Christ, oh! what honour it reflects on the gospel. God's grace is illustrated and magnified in the poverty and trials of believers. Saints bear up under every discouragement, believing that all things work together for their good, and that out of apparent evils a real blessing shall ultimately spring—that their God will either work a deliverance for them speedily, or most assuredly support them in the trouble, as long as he is pleased to keep them in it. This patience of the saints proves the power of divine grace."*

---

* Charles Haddon Spurgeon, *Morning and Evening: Daily Readings by C. H. Spurgeon* (Grand Rapids, MI: Christian Classics Ethereal Library, n.d.), reading for Morning, March 4, http://www.ntslibrary.com/PDF%20Books%20II/Spurgeon%20Morning%20and%20Evening%20Readings.pdf.

In the Beatitudes, Jesus gives us instructions for living a life oriented toward His kingdom; He describes its values and priorities. In this book, you will read about people who have embraced that orientation and aligned themselves with those priorities, which the world would find strange: selflessness, sacrifice, discomfort, humility. God's blessing flows through them and provides plenty where there is lack, love where there is hatred, forgiveness where there is offense, comfort where there is fear or pain, and wisdom where there is ignorance. Yes, the world can be a harsh and cold place, but the warmth of our God's love has the power to melt hearts of stone and bring restoration and reconciliation in the lives of people who surrender to Him.

I pray these stories will uplift you and give you hope, as they did for me. I pray that the deep, abiding joy of God's blessing will strengthen you with the hope that one day God Himself "will wipe away every tear from their eyes; there shall be no more death, nor sorrow, nor crying. There shall be no more pain, for the former things have passed away" (Revelation 21:4, NKJV). I pray that when you face adversity, you will recognize your divine appointment with blessing. No matter what valley you find yourself traveling today, the view from God's mountain will be glorious, and through His blessing we can, like Moses, receive a glimpse of the Promised Land.

—Céleste Perrino-Walker,
editor

Introduction

Mission Statement: It is the purpose of Versacare, Inc., to serve humanity by engaging in activities that will further the kingdom of God and restore the "image of God" in man. We believe that this fidelity to the gospel of Jesus urges us to emphasize human health and dignity and the search for knowledge.

There are hundreds of Adventist ministries around the world, each doing its part in showing the Father to those who do not know Him. While some of these ministries are quite prominent, many are unheralded and little known beyond the impact they make in the lives of those to whom they minister.

This book presents stories of lives changed due to the efforts of twenty-three such Adventist ministries. Included are stories from The Hope Channel, an official ministry of the General Conference, and Your Story Hour, which has blessed generations with its radio ministry. But also included are congregational and independent efforts by church members, all committed to improving the lives of those with whom they come in contact.

The common thread for all of these ministries and their stories is their association with, and past support from, Versacare, Inc., an independent foundation that has served Adventist ministries with financial grants since 1990. We are a self-funded lay organization, and our board includes both lay Adventists and present and former Adventist Church employees, all committed to furthering the kingdom of God and to restoring the image of God in those who are in need.

In Matthew 25, we are told that one day the Master will welcome us home by saying, "Well done!" Our prayer is that you are blessed by the stories told here and that if the work of any particular ministry speaks to your heart, you will follow the contact links provided to find out more about them, add them to your prayer list, and even donate to their work if the Holy Spirit moves you to do so.

—Thomas K. Macomber, JD,
president, Versacare, Inc.

*"Blessed are the poor in spirit,
for theirs is the kingdom of heaven."*

—Matthew 5:5, NIV

Bring-Your-Sibling-to-School Day

Amistad International

The Buddha's Smile School in Varanasi, India, is a little out of the ordinary. For starters, it provides education for the children of beggars and garbage collectors, many of whom are Bangladeshi refugees with no status in India, not even a caste—the hereditary classes of Hindu society with relative degrees of ritual purity or "pollution," which determine social status. Their children would not otherwise be able to go to school.

Varanasi is considered Hindu India's most holy city. The Ganges River flows through it, and Hindus try their best to go to Varanasi when they are dying, believing that if they manage to die in Varanasi, they can skip reincarnation. Not surprisingly, it is considered the city of death. But for the students of Buddha's Smile School, it is also a city of hope in the form of education. Here they learn to hope for a brighter future, for expanding opportunities, and for an escape from the prison of slum poverty.

The school began with a humble teacher, Rajan Kaur Saini, who provided education for sixty impoverished students crammed into a few makeshift classrooms built on her family's small city lot. Sixteen years ago, Amistad International got involved and helped build new classrooms. The project was the perfect opportunity for the organization, which serves impoverished people around the world, sharing knowledge and resources where they are needed. Helping Rajan educate and empower her students met their goal of enabling community leaders to teach, develop, and empower the rural poor so that they can participate in their own development.

Girls in Varanasi don't have the same opportunities as boys. Rekha, who is nine, comes from a refugee family of garbage collectors and lives in a stick-and-rag shanty. She started attending school at Buddha's Smile School in 2012, but when her baby brother was born in 2014, her mother forced her to stay home to help collect trash and care for the baby. Every time another baby is born into the family, the role of the older sisters is to stay home as caregivers while their mothers go out to work or, in the case of some mothers, drink alcohol in an attempt to escape their painful lives. Over the years, this scenario has stopped dozens of Buddha's Smile School girls from continuing their education. Soon Rekha joined

Bring-Your-Sibling-to-School Day

them, coming to school only once a week, dejection written all over her face.

To solve this problem, Amistad International came up with a creative solution: they built a day care center, another unusual feature of Buddha's Smile School, which allows the girls to bring their siblings with them to school every day. While their older sisters learn, the toddlers spend the school day in the day care center, a 950-square-foot space for play and child care. It features bathrooms, wash-up sinks, and mattresses for the children's naps. As an added incentive for parents, the tiny siblings are cleaned up, dewormed, and fed when they come to the day care center.

When the day care center opened, Rajan convinced Rekha's mother to allow her to bring her little brother to school. And Rekha's mother agreed.

"Rekha is so happy that she is back at school and that her brother is well cared for. She checks on him during the day to make sure he is OK," Rajan reported later to Rekha's mother. "One day, Rekha will be an independent woman and have children of her own who won't have to beg or collect trash for a living. I am sure of that."

Buddha's Smile School stands as a beacon, guiding children away from the desperation of poverty toward a brighter future of work and family. Children have this future because of the school's provision to honor their responsibilities by providing the day care center, which in turn allows them the freedom to pursue an education. For girls like Rekha, the obstacles to education are very real, forcing her to drop out of school to collect garbage and care for her new baby brother. It is only thanks to the day care center that she is allowed to come to school with her little brother in tow. A bright girl, Rekha is excited about her studies. With Rajan as her inspiration, she dreams of becoming a teacher one day.

Thirteen-year-old Sarita also faced serious challenges. She suffered from chronic malnutrition and hunger. Both her parents were alcoholics. She was often abused by drunken men in the nighttime streets. There is no protection on the streets for young girls whose parents are alcoholics, and Sarita tried her best to protect her siblings. Sadly, she learned to drink alcohol to help her fall asleep when she was hungry.

Even though her brothers were attending Buddha's Smile School, Sarita wasn't allowed to go to school. When Rajan asked, "Why don't you come to school, too?" Sarita replied to the question with sad perplexity, "But who will look after my baby brother?"

Now Sarita is attending Buddha's Smile School, and she brings her brother Raj to the day care center. Because the Buddha's Smile School children are often victims of feral dog bites, burns, and violence, the school provides medical care as well. The students also receive a daily nutritious meal that, for some, is their only meal of the day. Many of the students must beg or collect garbage before and after school to help their families survive. Sarita is often so tired from begging early in the morning that she sometimes falls asleep in class.

A Buddha's Smile School student brings her baby brother to the school's day care so that she can attend classes while her mother begs.

It is an uphill battle. The girls also face tremendous pressure from their parents, who are themselves beaten down by poverty and push them to beg for money or to work instead of going to school. In some cases, girls are married off as young as thirteen so that they won't be a burden on their families. One of the school's early teen girls was forced by her mother to marry a twenty-five-year-old man from a distant village. As is the Indian tradition, she went to live with her husband's family and be in service to them.

A few weeks later the man phoned his young wife's brother and told him to come and retrieve his sister because she was "ill." After collecting her, the brother called Rajan, the director of Buddha's Smile School, asking her what to do for his sister, who seemed very sick. Rajan took the girl to a doctor, who said she had been raped so violently by her husband that her internal organs were severely injured. Within twenty-four hours she was dead from marital rape.

Resisting age-old ways and expectations in order to pursue their dreams through Buddha's Smile School is difficult for girls, and for some it is impossible. But by educating girls in India and other countries and helping them attend school, Amistad International hopes to give them self-confidence and a sense of their rights as human beings worthy of dignity and safety on this earth.

These girls overcome so many challenges to get to school that Rajan is heartbroken when they miss classes. She knows that each additional year a girl attends Buddha's Smile School increases her chances for a brighter future. The new day care center at Buddha's Smile School is proving to be an excellent solution for these girls and their little siblings. And by meeting the girls at the point of their need, Amistad International is making it possible for them to live out their dreams and someday escape the clutches of extreme poverty.

The Brightest Light

La Sierra University Enactus

Gowri breathed in the dry air as she stood at the gate. It would be dawn soon, and already she knew it would be another day of record heat. But the best jobs, the only jobs, would go to those who arrived before the sun rose, and Gowri needed the work. Her name, *Gowri*, meant "bright," but standing there, she did not feel much like the bright morning light as she waited with dozens of others for the jobs to be passed out.

It had been more than a year since her husband had left the village, promising to return within a few days after finding work in the nearest city. But instead of returning as promised, he chose to leave his village life and village wife behind and start over without them. Gowri had been alone ever since, joining the many women like her in the village who went out each morning seeking work as day laborers. These women have no job security, no health-care benefits, and no compensation if they are injured at one of the farms or construction sites where the work is available. They have nothing except the promise of earning up to two dollars—enough to pay for two small meals—in return for a single, twelve-hour, or longer, workday. And even if they are some of the lucky ones who found work that day, there is no guarantee that they will find it tomorrow.

Today, like the day before, luck was not on Gowri's side, and she was passed over. As the sun rose over the state of Tamil Nadu in the south of India, Gowri wearily began walking to the next farm. By the time she returned to the village center that evening, it was already dark. A women's self-help group was meeting, and that night, university students from the United States were promising a chance for steady, daily income greater than that earned by a day laborer.

Four students from La Sierra University's Enactus Team, one of more than 1,600 university-based teams found in nearly forty countries that use entrepreneurial action to better communities, had traveled to India to launch the cow bank. The students stood quietly before the gathered women. Their team had committed to ten years of work to address challenges in education, health and wellness, economic opportunity, and environmental sustainability in the village. A year before, they had proved their commitment, doubling the capacity of the local school to educate five hundred more students. Today they were offering cows as loans to people struggling to find work.

The milk from a single cow could be sold for four dollars or more per day, double the earnings of a full day of labor. But purchasing a cow required $500, an impossible amount of money for a day laborer to save. The cow bank closed that gap. The cows were insured, contracts were in place to guarantee a market for the sale of milk, and veterinarian visits were included to support the cow's health and milk yield; everything had been researched and planned.

It was a sound model of social entrepreneurship and the perfect project to support future ideas. As each cow loan was paid for over time, the funds would be reinvested into more cows. But none of that was going to work unless the students could convince at least one person in the gathering of the village's self-help group to trust the team.

The women were speaking quietly among themselves. The team's translator shared with one of the students what they were saying:

"It's not possible; we are day laborers. That is all we ever will be," said a woman sitting in the front.

"I can't read or write my own name," said someone in the back. "No bank would ever give me a loan."

Just as the students began to lose hope, someone spoke up.

"I will do it," the oldest woman in the group said as she slowly stood. "And," she said as she turned toward the others around her, "if I can do it, so can these young ones, starting with her," she said, pointing directly at Gowri.

Before the night was over, twelve women had agreed to become cow owners and to work to turn the opportunity into a life-changing result.

One year later, the students returned to Gowri's town. For a full year, they had worked with local partners, farmers, government representatives, dairy owners, and others to fully implement the La Sierra University Enactus cow bank project. It had been a tremendous success. The new cow owners were earning more than twice what they had before and were able to sustain themselves and their families and even repay the loans sooner than expected. So, the students had returned prepared to sign up twice as many participants as the year before.

But again, like the year before, the new potential cow owners were filled with self-doubt.

"We can't," the women whispered back and forth to one another.

"You can," said a voice that pierced through the darkness like a bright light. "I

The Brightest Light 21

had nothing, I thought I was nothing; I was invisible," said the voice.

Gowri walked to the front as she spoke. The woman who was once ignored as an outcast was now recognized as a businesswoman in the village. Those who once shunned her now sought her advice. And her loan had already been fully repaid. She had no obligation to be there that night. And yet she was because she now knew that she, like the other women watching her intently, had value and that they needed what she had needed: one real opportunity. Today, just as she had been able to do a year before, they could take that opportunity and multiply the results many times over.

Before the end of the night, because of Gowri's choice to shine brightly and make a difference in the lives of others, every single woman present had joined the La Sierra University Enactus cow bank project.

Gowri, pictured with La Sierra University Enactus team member Anais Guth, became an advocate for the school's cow bank project in her hometown of Tamil Nadu, India.

By 2017, the students of the La Sierra University Enactus team had entered the seventh year of implementing their India Field Station model, a ten-year commitment that runs multiple projects in the rural communities surrounding Denkanikottai, India. To date, their cow bank project has lifted more than 125 families above a living wage. This, combined with multiple education projects, has allowed more than five hundred additional children to attend school, and other skilled labor training projects have increased daily wages among young women by an average of 400 percent.

Unintended Consequences

La Sierra University Center for Near Eastern Archaeology

Friedbert Ninow didn't know what he was getting into when he started his theological education at Marienhoehe Academy in Darmstadt, Germany. More interested in the gym and soccer field activities, Friedbert discovered that academics were a necessary burden if he wanted to go into ministry. Things changed when he and his wife spent a sabbatical in England, where they frequently visited the British Museum. Studying the numerous artifacts from the ancient Near East that related to the biblical narrative opened for him a new window into an ancient world. Suddenly he realized that the biblical text came out of a real world, and it was not the world that he had imagined from his children's Bible.

When he returned to Germany to continue his theological education, he immediately connected with the Old Testament professor, Udo Worschech. Professor Worschech had studied under noted Seventh-day Adventist archaeologist Siegfried Horn at Andrews University and had participated in a number of seasonal digs at the Tall Hisban (biblical Heshbon) archaeological excavation site. He had just started another archaeological project in Jordan on his own. He agreed to take Friedbert as a volunteer for his first big dig season at Khirbat al-Balu`a on the central Moabite plateau just east of the Dead Sea.

The very first morning in Amman, the call to prayer from a nearby mosque woke everyone with a start. Once they departed the modern capital of Jordan, they found themselves in the rural part of the land east of the Jordan river dotted with little villages and occasional Bedouin tents pitched in the fields along the highway. Their destination was a little Christian village not far from the site of the excavation, where they would live for the next several weeks.

Friedbert was excited about the potential of the project. Khirbat al-Balu`a was one of the largest sites in Transjordan from the Iron Age (the time of the biblical kings); all periods of occupation (early Bronze Age to middle Islamic period—fourth millennium B.C. to A.D. 1500) were represented in the excavation. Situated on the northeastern fringe of the plateau, Balu`a consisted of extensive

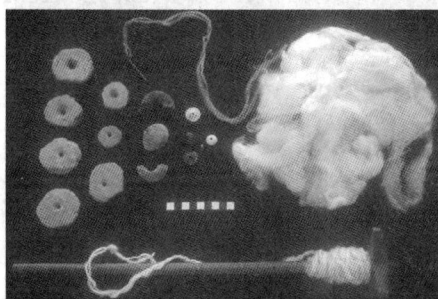

The Madaba Plains Project is an archeological research endeavor in Jordan that started in 1968 in Hisban and is administrated out of Andrews and La Sierra universities. They have three current dig sites—Tall Hisban, Tall al-`Umayri, and Tall-Jalul. *Top left:* Temple remains; photo courtesy Madaba Plains Project—`Umayri. *Lower left:* `Umayri textile spinning equipment. *Right:* Regional map.

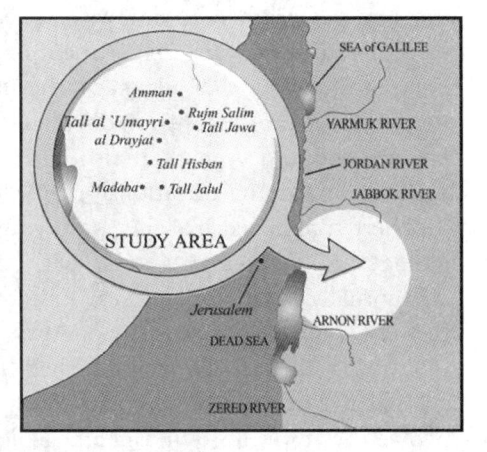

architectural remains. Due to its strategic location, this settlement guarded the northern access to the central Moabite plateau. The main site was strewn with basalt blocks of all sizes, stemming from the remains of houses and the city wall. Even from a distance, Friedbert's eye was caught by the characteristic silhouette of the *qasr* ("stronghold") originating from the late Bronze Age (circa 1300 B.C.) but rebuilt in later periods. The *qasr* appeared to have been the center of the older city in the western part of the site.

This older part of the city was enclosed by a casemate wall (two parallel walls separated by cross walls that, when filled with dirt, could create a defensive wall twenty feet thick), with its main gate facing east. During the latter part of the Iron Age, the city was extended toward the east with a new city wall encompassing about thirty-seven acres. Within the city, a great number of wall lines were still well preserved, and it was possible to trace many building complexes, streets, and other installations.

In 1930 Balu`a received special attention when the famous Balu`a Stele, an inscribed standing stone, was discovered. The stele was of black basalt with an irregular, conical-shaped top. Its face was divided into two parts: an upper panel, roughly one-third of the stele, with an inscription, and a lower panel—the remaining two-thirds—with an "Egyptianizing" relief consisting of three figures. Due to the badly preserved inscription, no satisfactory transliteration of the script had been produced so far. The stele had been tentatively dated to the thirteenth to eleventh centuries B.C. Based on textual evidence from Numbers 21:15–28 and 22:36; Deuteronomy 2:9, 18, 29; and Isaiah 15:1, Khirbat al-Balu`a can possibly be identified with the Moabite city of Ar. Professor Worschech started his project in 1986; Friedbert joined in 1987, and he returned more than twenty times over the next thirty years. The visits profoundly shaped his academic career and personal life.

The archaeological project also provided an opportunity for locals to earn some money and for the archaeologists to interact with them and their families. One of Friedbert's "workmen," Satar, was a twelve-year-old boy. He was the nephew of the representative of the Department of Antiquities of Jordan. Every project was required to have such a person on the staff for the duration of the project. Over the course of the season, Friedbert and Satar became friends. When the team returned the next year, Satar also returned to the site and requested to work in Friedbert's area. Their relationship grew over the years. As they worked together, Friedbert recognized in Satar a growing love for archaeology, a passion for his heritage, and a longing to preserve it.

Eventually Satar studied Near Eastern archaeology and finally became a representative of the Department of Antiquities; he was even assigned a couple of times to Friedbert's site, where he had begun as a youngster. He became a valuable partner in their project and was a fine example of how important it is to involve the community in the archaeology work. Friedbert came to realize that only through those relationships could they create a sense of trust and ownership among the local population by demonstrating respect for their heritage and making it something to treasure and value rather than a being simply a means of exploitation through destruction and looting.

Satar's uncle (their first representative) had worked for a number of years as their liaison to the Department of Antiquities, and he and his family also became Friedbert's close friends over the years. One of his daughters studied archaeology and at one point was the representative for their project. She later advanced into the office of the department, where she continues to serve as the public relations director for the entire department. One of her brothers was sponsored by Professor Worschech and his wife to attend Friedensau Adventist University and enroll in a master's program in international social development. He completed that program with a thesis titled "Human Rights in the Arab World." He went on to complete a doctoral program at the University of Erfurt, from which he graduated with a PhD degree. He now works as a lecturer at the University of Erfurt in the area of history of Western Asia.

Over the years, La Sierra University Center for Near Eastern Archaeology has provided field schools for a number of Jordanian archaeology students. Some of them have continued their education abroad and returned to serve in various capacities within the Department of Antiquities. Seeing those young women and men work for the preservation and development of their heritage is one of many unanticipated results that Friedbert couldn't have foreseen when he started as a volunteer on his first archaeological project back in 1987.

The Making of a Lady

Youth and Family Life Education Institute

When the Youth and Family Life Education Institute introduced a new program, Making of a Lady, at her school, Shanquaris was one of fifty girls who joined. The program had its roots in a wonderful girls' program initiated and sponsored at Houston Hill Junior High in Montgomery, Alabama, by then-faculty member Keesha Farris. The Youth and Family Life Education Institute began assisting Ms. Farris and the girls until she was transferred, and the program died for lack of a school sponsor.

However, the vision for reaching out and impacting the lives of girls and young women remained alive in the heart of the institute's executive director, Sandra Hawkins, a retired public-school educator. Ms. Hawkins studied the girls attending the school and determined they most needed training and mentoring in self-esteem, leadership, community involvement, character, and sisterhood education. Additionally, the girls were often abuse survivors, and they needed cultural exposure to positive people and activities outside their neighborhoods.

Program participants received summer scholarships to attend outdoor and performing arts camps as well as summer camps operated by the South Central Conference of Seventh-day Adventists. Attending camp was a novel experience for these kids, many of whom had never left the state of Alabama. Some had never been to the other side of town. Others had never been on a college campus, including the one where the performing arts camp was held during the summer.

Shanquaris lived with her mother, baby sister, and aunt in the Tract 6 community. For government census-taking purposes, the city is divided into tracts. Tract 6 was once home to neighborhoods filled with stately homes and a pristine park; that is, pristine until the park was desegregated. One day black people were declared eligible to access the park; that same night, trucks lined up to fill the pool with loads of cement. Today an open pavilion marks the spot where the park's pool was once located. Most of the residents who could afford to have moved out of the neighborhood.

As she participated in the Making of a Lady classes at her middle school, Shanquaris was quiet and smiled a lot.

Above: Shanquaris Brisker (front), Serena Brisker (baby sister and newest Making of a Lady family member), with Sandra Hawkins, YFLEI Director

Left: Shanquaris, high school JROTC officer

One day, she approached Ms. Hawkins after class and asked, "What church do you go to?"

Stunned, Ms. Hawkins told her. Neither she nor the volunteers had ever tried to speak to the girls about religion. Proselytizing would jeopardize their program.

Shanquaris announced, "I want to go to your church."

Ms. Hawkins visited Shanquaris's home and spoke with her mother, asking permission for Shanquaris to attend church. Her mother agreed. When Shanquaris arrived at church, she wasn't alone; she had brought her aunt and baby sister with her. Her mother had dropped them off.

Each summer, the Youth and Family Life Education Institute provided funds for students to attend the South Central Conference summer camps in Tennessee. Friendship Camp was the first time many students had been out of Montgomery to another state for such an event—or, for some, any event. That summer the institute was able to send Shanquaris and several other girls from her school to Friendship Camp. Shanquaris loved camp, and camp loved her. Instead of one week, she attended for two.

Later that summer, as part of her leadership training, Shanquaris made a presentation to the local school board. The school system, despite the community's protest, had closed Houston Hill Middle School, and the Making of a Lady program would either die along with the school or move on and live. As Shanquaris stood talking about her experience in the program that school year, Ms. Hawkins decided what would happen.

Shanquaris, with her beautiful smile, shy and quiet, who had apparently fallen in love with the program, was also moving on to high school. She represented the result of their effort to make an impact on the girls at her school that year. This talk was her first and last speech as a middle schooler. Just as Shanquaris moved on to high school, Making of a Lady would move on to another middle school in the city.

Eventually, Shanquaris joined the Junior ROTC (Reserve Officers' Training Corps) at her high school and became a leader. A few years later, Ms. Hawkins received an invitation to her high school graduation. When she celebrated graduation at church, her aunt and baby sister came with her. Shanquaris went on to join the Air Force.

One afternoon, Ms. Hawkins's doorbell rang. When she answered the door, she found a representative of the United States Air Force who questioned her about Shanquaris. Next came a phone call asking for an appointment for more in-depth questions. Ms. Hawkins learned that her former student was being considered for some type of top level security clearance. Shanquaris got the clearance.

They reunited a year later before her deployment for service in Qatar. They ate at a fast-food restaurant with Serena, Shanquaris's younger sister, who was now in seventh grade. As they chatted about the upcoming deployment and Ms. Hawkins's new girls' project, Serena listened. The new project would be a hands-on abbreviation of Making of a Lady's character, leadership, service, and sisterhood classes taught during the school year when the schools made more time available during the school day. Individualized assessments would also help girls determine their learning styles and work on conflict resolution issues in the context of their personality traits. This first-ever Girls' Leadership Workshop would also provide the opportunity to explore their interests in art, music, and the spoken word. At the end of the day, their student-driven show for parents and friends would synthesize all they had learned during the workshop.

Serena broke into the conversation with a request to participate in the workshop. Ms. Hawkins was thrilled and a warm feeling overtook her. For a moment she reflected on the humble beginnings of this ministry that had started in her home as a way to help the hurting kids she was seeing pass through her classroom. How it had grown! The institute had not only reached out to help make broken girls whole and whole girls, such as Shanquaris and Serena, better as they walked into womanhood but also reached into the community with programs that included, among others, community technology classes, public speaking training for students, and a literacy program conducted in elementary classrooms in the public school system.

When God called her to start the ministry, He had said, "What I have ordained, I will sustain," and Ms. Hawkins could clearly see His hand of providence, provision, and protection, not only in her own life but also in the lives of those she had been blessed to serve through the years.

Update: Shanquaris returned safely from Qatar and is now stationed in the United States. Serena attended the Girls' Leadership Workshop both years it has run, and she invited her best friend, who also attended.

The Next Step

Camp Ida-Haven

There was something peculiar about Patrick. Douglas Roe, a staff member working at Camp Ida-Haven, a Seventh-day Adventist Church–owned camp located on the shore of Payette Lake in McCall, Idaho, puzzled about the eight-year-old Rwandan refugee's curious behavior. He had come to Cub Camp with the assistance of a couple at his local church. They coordinated the details and helped kids get ready for their week-long adventure. Grants, church sponsorships, and Camp Ida-Haven's scholarship program made it possible for these kids to attend.

Patrick seemed to be enjoying his week at camp thoroughly except when he was in a crowd. In a small group, he seemed happy and fine; but in larger groups, he suppressed his joy. Finally, at the Thursday night campfire, Douglas decided to see whether he could find out why Patrick was so reserved at times.

He sat next to the boy and asked companionably, "I've noticed you don't smile a lot. Aren't you having a good time?"

Patrick's reply cut deep. "Have you seen my teeth?"

Douglas was so shocked at the revelation that he almost reeled. Patrick had four extra teeth, and their effect on his smile was debilitating to him. Douglas could easily imagine what Patrick must have suffered on a daily basis.

After camp was over, Douglas visited the local church to report on how their money had been used for scholarships, but he couldn't get Patrick and his self-consciousness out of his mind. Returning from the church, he prepared to enjoy the day off. The gates of the camp were closed, and he settled into an easy chair. His mind was busy with the challenge of Patrick's smile, which he hoped to be able to solve after a well-deserved nap.

Suddenly the doorbell rang.

Because it was his day off, the camp was closed, and the longed-for nap beckoned, he answered the door with less than his usual enthusiasm.

"The gates were closed, so we walked in!" the guests on the doorstep exclaimed. "Our daughter is going to attend camp here next summer, and she's a little nervous about it. We wanted to show her around and let her see what a great place this is so that she won't be scared of coming."

Douglas blinked in disbelief. Standing with the eight-year-old in question was her mother, who was a former staff member, along with her father, who was an orthodontist, and her grandfather, who was not only a camp supporter but also a dentist. It was as if God had deposited the answer to his problem directly onto his doorstep. During the tour intended to dispel the fear of the unknown for the little girl, Douglas made a deal for Patrick to visit the dentist to remove his four very pronounced extra teeth and then to see the orthodontist to have his smile made whole.

When Douglas ran into Patrick's pastor later, he said that the night Patrick found out that arrangements had been made to give him a new smile, the boy had prayed that he would be worthy of the gift. Following the transformation of his pearly whites, Patrick's personality bloomed. The happy, grinning boy even joined his church's choir.

Although most campers hail from the nearby Treasure Valley, other campers, like Patrick, arrive from faraway places including China, New Zealand, Alaska, and many other states in the United States as well. Estimates suggest that most people make critical decisions about God between the ages of eight and fifteen. Most of Camp Ida-Haven's campers fall in that age bracket. The camp's ministry of songs, skits, and messages, along with the powerful impact of a practical example demonstrated by staff they admire, all work together to create changes in the lives of young people that will be measurable only in eternity.

To reach more kids, Camp Ida-Haven decided to offer a week-long camp for special needs children. The medical costs and constant care place a heavy toll on those families, and Camp Ida-Haven wanted to offer a refuge from that challenge. They called it NeXt Camp because it was their next step. The camp was scheduled over the long Labor Day weekend.

The first year, they discovered, much to their dismay, that even with a skilled doctor on staff, parents of special needs children did not trust them with their kids. To make the camp work, they needed to invite the entire family to camp. Doing so would allow parents to monitor the program for their children and to meet and form bonds with other families facing similar challenges.

One family typified what became a familiar story for the families of campers with special needs. The husband and wife were attending NeXt Camp with their two children, ages ten and seven. The older boy had autism, and the younger one had cerebral palsy. On the second day of camp, the couple was able to leave their two boys with staff while they went for a ride on a sit-down personal watercraft. They returned ecstatic.

"This is the first time in ten years that we've had a vacation!" they exclaimed.

As a special memento of the families' camp stay, the staff produced a video record of each family's visit, which they presented to the families to enjoy until they returned the following year. The cost is covered by a grant, so there is no charge to the families, who already have enough challenges to manage. Each invitation to NeXt Camp comes from Camp Ida-Haven's contacts and references in the Boise area. Currently, just over ten families look forward with eager anticipation to their yearly visit to Camp Ida-Haven, and they have gone so far as to set up a Facebook page to keep in contact and support each other.

Portraying the love of God, regardless of differences, is Camp Ida-Haven's mission. Each camper they love and each family they assist gives them the opportunity to demonstrate the love God has for all His children as they take step after step, walking the road to the kingdom.

Sewing and Growing

Amistad International

Reginah Riton is an unusual Maasai girl. A determined young woman, she completed an eighth-grade education at the age of seventeen in 2016, no small feat in her culture—but there was no hope of further formal education for her. And there was great pressure on her to marry.

The Maasai tribe is one of the most impoverished tribes in East Africa. The Maasai are a dignified people who have maintained their traditional lifestyle and cultural identity despite the pressures of the modern world. While there is a certain nobility about the Maasai's dignity and determination to maintain this lifestyle, it means that at least 90 percent of Maasai girls are never educated due to the cultural practice of early marriage. Since a daughter becomes a member of her husband's family when she marries, often as early as thirteen years old, the biological family sees little benefit in educating a daughter. Instead, cattle and cash dowries are economic incentives for early marriage, and unmarried pregnancy is greatly feared because it is a disgrace and lowers the bride price. Women are chiefly valued by the number of children they have, so early marriage is the pathway to community respect.

Reginah sought an alternative path for her life; she was willing to buck cultural norms to determine her own destiny. She had heard something about the Grow Biointensive Agriculture Center of Kenya (G-BIACK) program, which trained rural girls in agriculture, sewing, and handcrafts. G-BIACK "sits on one acre of land ten miles east of Thika, north of the City of Nairobi. G-BIACK's land is the average size of a family farm in their region. The center is designed as a model farm for small-scale farmers. Student farmers have planted over 160 double-dug beds, growing different types of local food crops with organic compost. There are also chickens, rabbits, dairy goats, fish pond, bee-keeping, resource library for the community and nutrition classes. Amistad sponsors their program for at-risk teens who study for one year and learn food production, livestock care, sewing, and computer skills. Handcrafts are taught at the school, and the artist's products are sold in the center's store."*

---

* "Kenya," Amistad International, accessed September 26, 2018, https://amistadinternational.org/kenya/.

On her own initiative, Reginah wrote to G-BIACK cofounders Samuel and Peris Nderitu to ask to join the G-BIACK Girls' Empowerment Program. Peris was surprised and delighted. Impressed by Reginah's ambition, she invited her to apply. She was accepted, was sponsored by Amistad International for one year, and joined the others in the girls' dorm learning sustainable agriculture methods and teaching skills to ensure her future food security. She also learned life skills that will help her to succeed in adapting to a wider world as well as a variety of other income-generating skills, such as sewing and tailoring, cooking and baking, and computer literacy.

Statistically, an educated woman learns her rights and builds "the confidence and independence to stand up for them. She will choose whom to marry and when to marry. She will have fewer children, and they will be healthier and better educated than the previous generation. She will not circumcise her daughters. She will have economic security."*

Over the many years that Amistad has been working with the Nderitus, Amistad has learned to pay close attention when these community leaders have a new idea for reaching more youth. The Amistad investments are practical and fund low-risk projects, such as helping G-BIACK and other groups develop their farming, textile, baking, sewing, and computer programs for at-risk or HIV-positive youth. The vast majority of the sewing students, armed with a valuable skill, have either started their own sewing businesses or are working in a larger sewing enterprise.

Peris and Samuel are particularly concerned about the future of rural Kenyan girls who have little access to programs that teach how to grow more food on their family's small plot holdings and other practical job skills. They deal with very low-income families who face many problems. Most rural families do not have regular employment, relying on day-labor jobs when they can find them. Peris and Samuel strive to get them out of extreme poverty, but it is not easy because many of their students have only a very tiny piece of land that is too small to grow sufficient food.

At the top of Peris's wish list was a dormitory for rural girls. Having a dormitory would enable the faraway girls to attend training and have a safe place to stay at G-BIACK during their eighteen-month course. Their wish came true when they were able to build a dormitory with Amistad's financial support.

One of the sewing students from a rural area is Meryline Wekesa. Meryline is eighteen and the mother of a four-year-old son. She dropped out of school after ninth grade because her family was no longer able to pay the school fees. Her grandmother cared for her son while she attended G-BIACK's sewing and farming classes. "I know that God has big reasons for me to be here at G-BIACK,"

---

* "The Need," Maasai Girls Education Fund, accessed September 26, 2018, http://maasaigirlseducation.org/the-need/.

Sewing and Growing

Reginah Riton, a member of the Maasai tribe in East Africa, waters the garden at the Grow Biointensive Agriculture Center of Kenya program. There she learned agriculture, sewing, and handcrafting.

Meryline says. "I want to be a woman of empowerment, and I want to learn job skills. I really appreciate G-BIACK being here for me."

Esther Muthoni is another very serious student. She arrives at G-BIACK punctually at eight o'clock in the morning to study and learn for four hours. Then she leaves at noon to sell boiled eggs to construction workers during lunchtime. Returning to G-BIACK at three o'clock, she continues her studies in the afternoon. Esther is determined to provide a better life for her three children. "I never missed even a single class," she told a friend. "It's not because I don't have other things to do but because I love this school and what I am being taught. I dream of having a business where I can sell clothing and clothing accessories. This course has changed my life positively."

Esther went on to start a sewing business in Muguga, a few kilometers from G-BIACK. She also started a poultry business. In a bid to explore and expand her sewing business, she moved to the bigger city of Nyeri, where her business is doing well. Her children are in school too.

A large number of girls and women who have graduated from the sewing program are working as tailors. Some of them have started their own businesses; others have been employed by other tailoring shops, while even more are working at the export processing zone in Athi River, Kenya. When the G-BIACK sewing students graduate, the majority of them want to set up their businesses in towns where the population is high because that is where they can make the most money.

As each new student is educated and empowered to make decisions for her life, she creates a future that honors the dignity and determination of her ancestors while providing herself with the tools to live a happier, more fulfilled life. Through education, the future of women in Kenya can improve dramatically, with each generation building upon the last, seamlessly stitching the past to the present.

*"Blessed are those who mourn,
for they will be comforted."*

—Matthew 5:4, NIV

An End and a Beginning

Project Patch

Jeff* was smart—almost too smart for his own good.

School wasn't hard, but he was failing. He would have passed if all he had to do was take tests. He was failing because he wouldn't do his work, or if he did do it, he'd lose it or "forget" to turn it in.

Jeff was an only child, and his dad hadn't been a part of his life for years. His mom had her career, made great money, and wasn't home much. They lived separate lives. She worked; he played video games, which he loved. She wanted to spend time with him one-on-one on weekends, but they didn't have any interests in common, and he hated talking, with her or anyone else.

Eventually, Jeff's mom couldn't get him to do anything. He wouldn't get out of bed in the morning. She'd coax, threaten, punish, and bribe, but he wouldn't budge. She'd be forced to leave for work, hoping he'd go to school. The situation took a major turn when she followed up on her threats by taking all the video games and computers out of the house. He screamed at her and became physically out of control. She was terrified. She knew something had to change for her safety and for Jeff's future.

She started asking people she trusted, and they suggested she look at Project Patch, a Christian therapeutic residential program for teens. At first she was nervous because residential care seemed like something only for hardened kids, the type who were getting in trouble with the law and doing drugs. Then she learned more about Jeff's needs and discovered that Project Patch was a place for therapy, learning responsibility, gaining friends, and learning to serve others. She was told that the boys' program used a combination of methods to help boys gain understanding, positive relationships, skills, and motivation to move forward. She was finally sold on Project Patch when she learned they had an accredited school on campus that helped kids reengage with learning.

Jeff arrived in Idaho on a cold spring day. He was fuming because his mom had only told him about the school part and had left out all the information

---
* Not his real name.

An End and a Beginning

Teens participate in therapy, service, schoolwork, and chapel services at Project Patch.

about therapy and no electronics. Ironically, what made him angriest about going to Project Patch was that he never had a chance to say goodbye to his friends. He was furious because they needed him and wouldn't know what had happened to him. The staff suggested that his mom could let them know, but Jeff said that was impossible because the only way to communicate with them was through the video games, and his mom didn't know how to use them.

Jeff's only friends were online. He'd spent hours with them completing gaming missions. They depended on one another. But Jeff couldn't tell anyone much about them other than the characters they played in his virtual world. He couldn't confirm age, gender, or even whether they really knew him or just the role he played in their game.

Being with a group of real, live boys was torture for Jeff. He didn't like to talk, he didn't like to do chores, and he hated sports. He decided the best way to get out of Project Patch was to treat it like the challenge of a game, take on a role, and work through the levels.

He started by deciding to "become" a Christian. He thought that if he made a big deal about giving his life to God that the staff would see it as the major change he needed and allow him to go home. It didn't work. Staff encouraged him to grow spiritually but wouldn't allow Jeff to manipulate them, especially not by using God's name for insincere reasons.

Jeff then decided that the staff would make it easier on him if he became an outgoing athlete. He tried his best at every sport and went out of his way to be social. He put on a smile and performed to the best of his abilities. He soon learned two important things. First, getting healthy made him feel better. Second, spending time with the guys learning how to play a sport felt great.

It didn't get him home, but it started to awaken something he had tried to hide for a long time.

Underneath his anger and hidden in the middle of his isolation, Jeff was a lonely and scared little boy who desperately wanted someone to care. Things began to change for him when he started to do things that he hadn't done for a long time. First, he allowed himself to be quiet and think. He was used to noise and distraction, and he decided to try instead to listen and learn. Second, rather than attempting to handle everything by himself, he wanted to connect with real people and accept support from them. Finally, he chose to feel. He decided not to play a role but to be himself and respond to his true feelings.

Jeff didn't go through a fast transformation. When things got tough, he slipped back easily into role-playing and avoidance. But over time, his transformation deepened. Jeff's journey was marked by moments of pain that he chose to face rather than to avoid. Being surrounded by a dorm full of caring male staff made him wonder how his dad could just walk away and never miss him.

He had chosen video games and isolation as his defenses against pain. These idols had stopped helping him and had instead enslaved him. Without them, Jeff mourned initially. And that's when he discovered something wonderful. God took his pain and sadness and used them to awaken his deep longing to be loved, for things to be made right, and for peace. After being in the youth program for nine months, Jeff asked whether he could pray during worship time. He wasn't showing off or manipulating. He believed and wanted God to be his source of life.

Jeff discovered a comfort that video games or even parents could never give.

He returned home after fourteen months at the Project Patch youth program. He finished high school, made good friends, chose to play sports, and is now in college. Jeff's mother and the staff at Project Patch are grateful for the blessings God provided in his life and for the privilege of seeing the transformation from addiction to mourning to comfort and growth.

The Worst of Times

The Unforgettables Foundation

In March of 2012, Jennifer Zambrano and her husband, Michael, found out that Jennifer was pregnant with not one, not two, but three babies—*triplets*! Jennifer wanted to be happy, but she was scared. She knew the risks of a multiple pregnancy. During her pregnancy, she and Mike visited the Neonatal Intensive Care Unit (NICU) at Loma Linda University Medical Center, knowing she'd deliver early and that their girls would probably have a NICU stay—a short one, they hoped.

On August 19, 2012, Makayla, Melaina, and Maya entered the world at twenty-six weeks, a full fourteen weeks before they were due. Makayla and Melaina were only one pound, six ounces each while Maya, their "big" girl, was one pound, seven ounces. They were itty-bitty. Jennifer was sure that if she had been allowed to hold them, they would have each fit in the palm of her hand. All three girls were rushed to the NICU the morning of their birth and put on ventilators because they could not breathe on their own. Jennifer was recovering from a C-section, so she wasn't able to see her daughters until late that night.

Because they were so small, she couldn't hold them; they were connected to many machines, tubes, and wires. Their skin was so thin that she could see through it. Each day they struggled to stay alive.

Very late one night, the Zambranos received a call from a nurse. She told them that Maya wasn't doing well and that they should come to the hospital immediately. When they arrived, they learned that Maya was having a hard time breathing, even while intubated. Many doctors, each with a different specialty, surrounded her. Staff poked needle after needle into her tiny body before she was diagnosed with necrotizing enterocolitis, or NEC, a disease that often affects the intestines of premature infants.

The next day she had surgery to remove the liquid that was filling her belly and to place a vacuum-assisted wound closure system (VAC) in her belly to stop the bloating of her entire body. She made it through the surgery like a champ and then took a couple of days to recover. Three days later, on September 30, she had another surgery to remove the VAC and to remove parts of her intestine that had died. She made it through that surgery too.

Jennifer and Mike stayed in the waiting room with the rest of their family waiting for the all clear so that they could see their baby girl. One of their favorite nurses came to get them, but the look on her face told them immediately that something was wrong. The nurse explained that Maya had made it out of surgery, but while in recovery she stopped breathing. She said they had done all they could to help her.

When Jennifer got to her baby, a doctor and some nurses surrounded Maya, still trying to breathe air into her little body. Slowly it began to sink in: her baby was gone. There was nothing she could do to bring her back. There were no words to explain the feelings she had at that exact moment. To say she was devastated would have been an understatement. No one who hasn't lost a child of their own can understand the emotion that goes through a mother who realizes there is nothing she can do to save the life of her child.

While mourning the death of their baby girl, the Zambranos had to plan a funeral, and they still had two daughters fighting for their lives in the NICU. It was the hardest time of Jennifer's life. Her faith was tested, and her will was hanging by a thread, but she knew that she had to stay strong and present for Makayla and Melaina.

Neither Mike nor Jennifer was working at the time because they needed to be available for their daughters. Bills were piling up, which added to the stress caused by the financial burden of paying to lay their daughter to rest while also taking care of Makayla and Melaina. They didn't have the emotional energy to consider where they were going to get the money. They simply longed to mourn without the worry.

When they went to the mortuary, the woman who helped them told them about The Unforgettables Foundation.

"It's a nonprofit organization set up to make it easier for families who need assistance with burial expenses for their child," she explained. "They might help you. It's worth a try."

The Zambranos filled out an application, and a few days later, The Unforgettables Foundation sent a check to cover a portion of Maya's funeral expenses. For that, they were profoundly thankful. The financial aid helped, but knowing there were people out there who understood the need that families have during the worst time in their lives was incredibly comforting.

Jennifer vowed to keep Maya's memory alive, but she wasn't ready to do something concrete about it until three years later when she realized that The Unforgettables Foundation was based only ten miles from her house. She felt the need to volunteer, to tell Maya's story, and to let people know how much the foundation's assistance had helped her family focus on their children instead of worrying about the financial burden of the funeral. She knew she would be forever grateful for the volunteers and donors who make such a great impact on the many families the foundation helps each year.

When she saw an ad for a part-time office assistant position listed at The Unforgettables Foundation, she decided to apply. When she met Tim Evans, the chaplain at Loma Linda University Children's Hospital and founder of The Unforgettables Foundation, she told him that she was happy to have the opportunity to give back to the charity that had helped honor her baby girl. The Zambranos, who live in Highland, California, attend fundraisers and speak to audiences about how the spiritual and financial support they received from the foundation was a tangible sign of caring. They stress that when you don't quite have the funds to afford a simple, timely, dignified funeral for your child, it adds insult to the profound injury of your baby's death.

To assist and partner with grieving families, The Unforgettables Foundation grants about $100,000 each year, most of it to families who will struggle for years to survive in the real fight with death and dying that is waged every day in every community.

Back From Broken

Thunderbird Adventist Academy

Renji Moreno had been raised Catholic, and throughout his young life, while he had always believed in God, he had never had a truly personal connection with Him. To him, God seemed about as personal as George Washington. He had seen paintings of the first president; he knew there were historical landmarks, documentaries about him, and proof that he had existed. But Renji had never met him and didn't have any connection to him.

Renji had grown up in an Asian household in Guam, born to a Japanese mother and a Filipino father, who was a committed Catholic. To his father, Renji's baptism into the Catholic church was a priority. But his mother, being traditional Japanese, didn't see it the same way. Still, both resolved that Renji should attend a religious private school. Though his parents agreed on this point, Renji wasn't interested.

The first school he attended was a Catholic school. The school itself had great intentions and high standards for its educational excellence. But Renji had many problems at school. His teachers degraded, humiliated, and embarrassed him in front of his peers. The negative effects of the teachers' influence were so great that he was scared to ask anyone for help, not his peers or even his parents. His studies suffered for it.

His peers believed the stereotype that because he was from an Asian household, his family had high standards for him and expected the best. But for Renji, it was not just a stereotype; it was also true. He was grateful that he had been born into an educated family who had taught him how to read and write properly, but as his grades plummeted, so did his heart. He knew he was letting his parents down.

Renji didn't have a relationship with God that would have allowed him to pray for his situation to get better. He wasn't sure whether his parents would believe him, either, if he confided in them. They were divorced now and had other things to think about. They seemed to think he was like so many kids who just wanted to stay home and goof off. Since they didn't know the cause of his troubles, they believed he was making excuses. Only Renji knew that he wasn't dumb or unteachable; he just couldn't learn in such a hostile environment.

While he was still living in Guam, his mother met a good but stern man who eventually became his stepfather. He, too, was Catholic and had a strong faith in God. When Renji was eleven years old, the family moved to Tiffin, Ohio, where Renji once again found himself in a Catholic school. The teachers were nicer, but Renji had been badly burned the first time and couldn't trust his teachers. There was, however, one compensation: he fell hard for the most gorgeous girl he had ever seen. She didn't really like him back, but Renji was so infatuated with her that it hardly seemed to matter as long as she was nearby.

His world came crashing down two years later when his stepfather told him they'd be moving to Arizona. Renji couldn't work up any enthusiasm for the move. By that time, he'd made friends, and there was the biggest crush of his life to consider. How could he leave her? But there was no choice, and by the next school year, he found himself in the town of Ehrenberg, Arizona.

Instead of a Catholic school, Renji's parents enrolled him in a public school, and he hated it, not because it was a public school but because the school, in general, was terrible. Renji wondered whether the teachers were even qualified to teach. His mother saw how unhappy he was and told him about a school that a coworker's daughter attended.

"It's a boarding school," she said hesitantly. "It's called Thunderbird Adventist Academy."

Located on the site of a World War II pilot training facility, Thunderbird Adventist Academy's founding aim was to develop the spiritual, mental, and physical faculties of its students. They were passionate for their students to excel by experiencing Jesus, learning to communicate clearly and think critically, embracing service and citizenship, and learning to live healthfully in body and mind. Their academic offerings surpassed his wildest expectations and included honors courses, college credits, and even private pilot training and certified nursing assistant programs.

Renji was intrigued and decided to take a tour of the school. Immediately he was hooked. He could tell Thunderbird had a better education system than the schools he had attended previously. He was fourteen and enrolled at Thunderbird as a freshman. Little did he know that his religious journey was about to get rocky very fast.

Renji "believed" in God, but he still didn't have any connection with Him. He prayed—but without any real intention. As he progressed through his sophomore year, he became an agnostic. His junior year caused him to hit a rock spiritually. He was pummeled by many problems that almost caused him to break. Among them was the girl he'd been so smitten with. She had promised to keep in touch, but she didn't return his phone calls. Then his father, who still lived in Guam, developed cancer.

Throughout his valley of shadows, he talked to people he looked up to, such as his dean and the teachers he trusted most. The teachers at Thunderbird were the only teachers he had ever met who not only were caring but also looked out for their students and acted in a Christlike manner. He felt so broken that he couldn't believe they never lost their cool and yelled at him. Instead, they encouraged him and told him that he was strong and capable.

Even so, by the week of finals at school, Renji was so discouraged that he had decided he was done with Christianity. He wasn't even planning to return for his senior year. However, his Bible teacher assigned the class a project on how they saw Jesus working in their lives. Because he loved his teacher so much, Renji wanted to do his best and turn in a great final project.

He had no idea what to do until he began to think about what would have happened to him if he hadn't gone to Thunderbird. An idea began forming in his mind. He called a friend from Ohio and asked how his crush was doing.

"Ah, man, she's hanging out with the wrong people, and I hear she's smoking marijuana now."

Renji felt a chill chase down his spine. He realized that being the type of person he was, he would have joined her, hoping she'd notice him. And if he had, he would have disappointed and dishonored his parents, and in all likelihood, he would have gotten in trouble. Because he'd been at Thunderbird, he'd been spared.

Thinking back over his time at Thunderbird, he also realized all the things he would have missed out on if he hadn't been there: being part of a music group, being part of an acrobatics team, demonstrating his love of martial arts. His teachers had shown him that he was capable of things he'd never dreamed of until then. They saw what he had always known: he wasn't unteachable or dumb.

Renji realized that he was incredibly grateful for all the different people he had gotten to know during his time at Thunderbird, for the brotherhood and sisterhood of the dorms and all his wonderful, caring, supportive teachers. He realized that God had brought him there for a purpose and helped him every step of the way. That was when he gave himself fully to God, accepting Him and believing in Him. Renji knew he would be eternally grateful that God had been there for him from the beginning, even if he hadn't known it at the time.

He not only found the material for his project but also discovered the answer to the question that was his life.

Little Girl Lost

Adventist Health International

In 2014, an Ebola crisis struck West Africa. Ebola, a horrible hemorrhagic virus that is highly contagious and deadly, raged like fire through Sierra Leone where little Rachel lived. She watched her mother and two of her sisters die from the disease. Victims of Ebola literally bleed to death internally. One day they were fine and healthy, and just a few days later, they were dead. Rachel was six years old.

The first thing she noticed was that she was cold. The trouble was, Sierra Leone is tropical, and it was never that cold. Rachel quickly sickened, and just a couple of days after first becoming ill, she was unconscious. By that time Sierra Leone had established Ebola treatment centers (ETCs) around the country, and when a new case was suspected, special ambulances were dispatched to pick up the patient and transport them to the nearest ETC. For some reason known only to God, the ambulance passed many ETCs and brought Rachel to Waterloo Adventist Hospital, fifty kilometers away. Because Ebola was so contagious, her family was not allowed to go with her.

It was near the end of the crisis, so by the time Rachel was admitted to the hospital, all the Ebola victims there had either died or been discharged. And so it was that Rachel was gently placed on a bed in the red zone of the hospital, the only patient there. All ETCs were divided into green and red zones. Green zones were "safe," there were to be no Ebola patients in those areas; the contagious patients were all confined to the red zone.

Because she was unconscious, she could not eat or drink, so she received fluids through a vein and was started on antibiotics to treat the secondary infections that often come with a viral infection. To care for Rachel, James Abu, the treating provider, had to enter the red zone wearing his personal protective equipment—a heavy, thick, rubber and plastic suit that covered every square millimeter of his body to protect him against any chance of coming in contact with the deadly virus. It takes only a few viral cells to start an infection, and most patients have a viral load of millions in each drop of blood. The staff had to limit their time in the red zone to two hours simply due to dehydration issues; they sweat so much in their suits that the large plastic boots they wore would be full of sweat by the time they removed them.

For two days, each time Mr. Abu checked on Rachel, she was in her bed, unconscious. He made sure she was receiving her medication and that she was kept hydrated and turned. The staff at the hospital was determined to do all that was possible to save this last little victim. They diligently prayed for her, asking for God's healing power, as they did for all their patients. Mr. Abu's heart ached to see this little one so ill. The only good thing was that she was asleep and no longer suffering.

On the third day, after a two-hour break, Mr. Abu painstakingly donned his equipment and returned to the red zone to check on his little charge. Her bed was empty! Mr. Abu searched the ward; no Rachel. He called for her; he looked under the beds; he looked in the closets and cupboards. He went outside the ward and looked along the fence and toward the gate. Rachel was nowhere to be found. He could not figure out where the unconscious little girl had gone. Had her family found out where she was and come and taken her? Had she died and someone else had taken the body? Where was his patient?

So, he searched again, looking in every nook and cranny, in every corner of every ward. Finally, he found her sound asleep, half on and half off another bed in the central receiving hall of the hospital. She had come out of her coma and walked through the hospital, all alone, until she had gotten tired and tried to crawl up onto the bed, where she fell asleep.

He could only imagine what had gone through the little girl's mind when she woke up. She had passed into unconsciousness at home and woken up in a strange, huge building with lots of empty rooms and empty beds with not another living soul around. The next time Rachel woke up, it was to the sight of a creature covered from head to toe in a space-suit-looking rubber jumpsuit—definitely not human. Eventually, James was able to calm the frightened little girl with a favorite canned drink he had saved for himself, and she drifted off to sleep again.

Although she was still very ill, Rachel was not one to give up easily. She battled bravely for three weeks and was finally discharged, alive and healthy, and reunited with her father, the only one left of her family. The prayers of James Abu and the staff at Waterloo Adventist Hospital had been answered. The survival of one little girl helped to offset their choice to sacrifice their safety and continue to serve their community while around them many medical centers had closed during the height of the Ebola crisis. During the crisis, three staff members at Waterloo Hospital had contracted Ebola, and only one survived. As they voluntarily risked their lives to work throughout the crisis, they spread the gospel through the ministry of healing.

While the bodies of the survivors have recovered, the scars of Ebola will last much longer. The mental scars of those who were ill and survived and of those who lost many members of their families to the awful disease continue to haunt them. The survivors suffer from guilt because they survived and others did not. They returned home to stigmatization, shunned by family, friends, and coworkers who were afraid of them and sometimes angry with them. The epidemic affected the country in other ways: it devastated the economy, hurting industry, mining, and tourism, causing unemployment, inflation, and increasing poverty in an already poor nation. Although Ebola is no respecter of age, it was often the children who suffered the most. They were the most vulnerable, and many either died or were left as orphans.

Adventist Health International supports Waterloo Hospital in its mission to provide high-quality, mission-focused health care in Sierra Leone. Adventist Health International is a nonprofit corporation focused on upgrading and managing mission hospitals by providing governance, consultation, and technical assistance to a number of affiliated Seventh-day Adventist hospitals throughout Africa, Asia, and the Americas. The hospital is staffed by many indigenous Adventist health professionals who see themselves as missionaries to their local community. Their work is more than a job; it's a calling. And they strive to make a difference, one little lost girl at a time, no matter the personal cost.

This story is adapted from a blog by Scott and Bekki Gardner. Scott is a general surgeon and Bekki is a registered nurse. They serve as missionaries in West Africa; Scott is the medical director of Waterloo Adventist Hospital and Bekki the supervisor of clinical services and materials management. Read more on their blog at https://gardners2koza.wordpress.com.

The Unexpected

The Unforgettables Foundation

Dalila Hernandez Magana never expected that the year 2003 would bring her anything but happiness and joy with the anticipated birth of her baby. Her boys were in school and doing well; her church family was fine. March 24 was her son Sergio's birthday. He was her second-born son and would be turning fifteen. She was eager for him to return home from a weekend of spending time with his dad so that she could give him his presents. When he arrived early enough, she was delighted.

He opened the gifts, and then, after a while, he set them aside.

"I'm going to go see my friend in the front of the apartment building," he announced.

"OK, but don't leave the premises," Dalila warned. "Or, at least, if you're going to leave, let me know first."

Sergio agreed and left to visit his friend. Not long after, he called to tell her that his friend was going to the store and asked if he could tag along.

Dalila gave him permission and didn't give it another thought until there was a terrible pounding on her front door. Her oldest son, José, whom everyone called Jojo, answered the door and as if from a long distance away, Dalila heard a voice urgently explain that Sergio had been hit by a car in front of the apartment.

"Come quickly!"

Dalila and Jojo ran to the scene, where Dalila struggled to take in what she was seeing. Sergio lay on the pavement bleeding from the head and surrounded by paramedics who were working desperately to save his life. Nearby, a helicopter waited at the grounds of the high school to airlift him to the hospital, but he couldn't hold on that long. He passed away while they were still en route.

Dalila was allowed to spend time with him, to say her goodbyes. But there were no answers to her questions as she cried over her son. "My baby, my baby! Why? Why!"

Dalila slipped into the darkness of anger and grief. Friends and family took care of funeral preparations because she was too upset to manage them. But life would not wait for her to process her grief. A month after losing one son, she brought her seventh baby, Julian, into the world on April 26, her oldest son's birthday. Dalila tried to be happy, but she was faking it, not wanting to disappoint her family and burden them with her grief.

Soon it was school vacation, and Jojo left to spend some time visiting his dad in Porterville. Dalila was glad he could leave and get away from the sorrow. She was beginning to think that he was taking his brother's death harder than she had realized. Lately, he had been telling people that he wanted to go with his brother and join him on the "other side."

On September 18, 2003, not quite six months after his brother died, Jojo was out with friends. The car he was in skidded on the edge of the road before flipping several times and landing on its hood. Three of the teens were injured, but alive. Jojo was not one of them. Because no one knew who he was, Jojo was labeled a "John Doe," and authorities were preparing to send his body to San Diego. Someone called to inform Dalila, and her family arrived to drive her to the coroner's office to identify Jojo's body.

Sergio and José (Jojo)

Once again, Dalila faced the devastating loss of a child. "Why me? Why?" she asked herself over and over, stunned and broken in her grief. Her heart fell, and coldness washed over her, numbing her to the pain. She didn't know where to turn.

Again, people pitched in to help. She mourned so deeply that she wasn't able to help with funeral arrangements at all. Family and friends took care of the service and put out donation boxes to help with expenses. It wasn't until later that she came across a box of sympathy letters and discovered one that struck her. It was a letter of condolence from The Unforgettables Foundation, which had sent donations to help bury her boys. The name and logo stayed in her mind.

One day many years later, she was invited to the annual Women's Show Health Expo, where she came across a booth featuring the same name and logo as the one on the condolence letter. She stood there, transfixed, her eyes filling with tears as she stared at the logo on the banner.

Tim Evans, the founder of The Unforgettables Foundation, was staffing the booth. "Do you know about our charity?" he asked gently.

She nodded, and after a long silence, she said, "Yes, I do. You helped me fourteen years ago. I lost two children in the same year, and your group helped me with the burial cost both times."

Stunned, Evans, a former chaplain at Loma Linda University Children's Hospital with thirteen years of experience in dealing with devastating situations, spoke with Dalila as the conference bustled around them. At the conclusion of her story, she expressed her gratitude for The Unforgettable Foundation's help and shared how she and Julian, the son she was carrying when she lost Sergio, were pursuing Sergio's dream of someday becoming an NFL player. As Julian grew up, he had seen pictures of his older brother and, in asking questions about him, discovered his brother's dream. Now a high-schooler, Julian played football while Dalila volunteered as a team mom, arranging concession sales for the football season and serving as a medic for the team. Together they worked to fulfill Sergio's dream.

When parents like Dalila receive *the* knock or phone call, they never expect that their lives are about to change irrevocably in a single heartbeat. A beloved child has died, and on top of the enormity of that impact, the impressive costs associated with the burial or cremation come as an extra kick in the gut. Helping already struggling families to cope with the profound loss that accompanies the death of a child is a key part of The Unforgettable Foundation's charity mission. The foundation hears their calls for help and strives to follow Jesus' example when responding to parents who have lost their child with compassion, empathy, and practical assistance.

*"Blessed are the meek,
for they will inherit the earth."*

—Matthew 5:5, NIV

The Nick of Time

Project Patch

Lisa has a story—the kind that's hard to hear and impossible to forget.

She arrived at Project Patch Youth Ranch the same day men were driving across the country to pick her up from her home. They had been grooming her online for months, and she was excited about the life of "freedom" they had promised her.

Her life consisted of three parts: the part she lived before being adopted by her grandparents, her life after adoption, and the painful spiral that led her to Project Patch.

For Lisa, the knocks started early. First graders love school, and Lisa was no exception. She loved being at school, but she missed one hundred days during that school year. It was hard to get to school when she had to take care of her little brothers. She was forced to do things around the home that her biological parents should have been doing. She would scrounge for food, and when there wasn't any, she'd hunt through the house for loose change and take her brothers to the store, where she bought what she could. Out of necessity, she learned to cook. But since there was no one to teach her, she had burns and cuts from learning through trial and error.

Her biological parents were addicts and more concerned about getting high than keeping their kids safe. There were always people in her home, and her biological parents were in no fit state to protect her or her little brothers.

Lisa's grandparents changed her world when they adopted her and her brothers. For the first time in her life, she had a real bed with sheets and blankets and a room full of pretty things. She had food and wasn't responsible for her brothers' medication and protection.

Lisa had lived in a home with people whom she had called her dad and mom, but they hadn't cared for her, protected her, or sacrificed for her. Her adoption gave her real parents who cared for her for the first time in her life. She no longer had grandparents; instead, they became her parents. Lisa was discovering the wonder of adoption, in which *Dad*, *Mom*, and *parent* finally started to make sense based on love, commitment, and faithfulness.

She liked having people who cared and looked out for her but didn't like being treated like a kid; she wasn't used to it. She liked to play but also found it hard to play. She wanted to mother her brothers, and it took time for her and her new mother to settle into their roles. Although she was only seven when her grandparents adopted her, Lisa struggled with being a kid and letting them be her parents.

Those elementary school years were a fairly peaceful time, especially compared to her traumatic early years. She had counseling and people to talk to, though she didn't share too much. The way she saw it, she had life figured out. She hated being treated like a child and couldn't wait to get out on her own.

Her painful downward spiral started when she was twelve. She was called to be a witness against someone who had harmed her and was trying to get out of prison. She showed great poise and bravery on the witness stand and was pivotal in making sure the person would never get out of prison. But those days of testifying reawakened painful memories she had worked hard to forget. She started having nightmares and couldn't sleep. That was when she started sneaking out at night and doing whatever she could to make the pain stop.

Drugs and sex were freely available, and she began repeating the choices her biological parents had made. Her adoptive parents were worried and eventually sent her to a detox camp. There she discovered freedom from drugs and a new relationship with Jesus Christ.

But getting off drugs proved to be much easier than getting out of negative relationships. Lisa's spiral resumed as she spent time online engaging with older men. It was this dangerous online and sexual behavior that finally prompted her mom to call Project Patch, hoping the Therapeutic Residential Treatment Program for Girls could help her daughter.

When Lisa arrived at Project Patch, she was sixteen years old, and though she was a pretty girl, her eyes were cold and her face expressionless. She was withdrawn and eerily quiet most of the time, but occasionally she would explode in anger, especially at the girls' dorm staff. She hadn't told anyone about her plan to leave with the men who were coming to get her. Only later, after many months of building trust, did Lisa share how close she had been to running away with those men.

Lisa's time at Project Patch wasn't easy. Being away from home at a therapeutic residential program was difficult. It was an intense time of having to think about hard things and face the reality of choices and behavior. She thought the other girls were immature and annoying. She wanted to fake things so that she could go home and get on with her life.

Yet, she started to change and long for deeper change. She started to care for herself and build relationships with other girls and staff. She reached out to her parents and allowed them to be the parents she desperately needed. Her faith continued to grow, and she discovered God was faithful in helping her face her memories and her fears as well as helping build trust again.

The Project Patch youth program campus is located in the mountains of southwest Idaho.

Lisa graduated Project Patch with a smile on her face and a sparkle in her eyes. She was proud of her accomplishment and ready to finish school. Things weren't perfect going home, but now she had the tools to deal with life's challenges without drugs, sex, and dangerous relationships.

Within months of graduating, Lisa, her parents, and her brothers attended the Family Experience for recent graduates from the Project Patch girls' program. The program was designed to help the whole family, not just Lisa. They spent the weekend building their family skills and doing challenging activities. It was Lisa's chance to share the Project Patch experience with her parents and brothers. The focus wasn't on Lisa but on the whole family.

On the last afternoon, the family gathered rocks and buried a copy of their new family covenant. The covenant was a document that captured their values, dreams, and plans. No one in their circle would have thought forming a new family would be as difficult as it had been. Buying beds, clothes, and food had been the easy part. Learning to trust, communicate, and heal was the hard part. The rock pile symbolized what they were building together: a foundation for strong life and love.

Lisa doesn't have an easy story, but it's a good story, one of a girl who had every reason to give up and didn't. A story about a girl who felt all alone but wasn't. A story of what is possible when people get together and partner to make an eternal difference in the life of a precious child.

Breaking the Cycle

Holbrook Indian School

Kill the Indian. Save the man.
—*Capt. Richard Pratt, 1892,
on the education of Native Americans*

Jovannah Poor Bear was desperate to escape the life of poverty and abuse she knew on South Dakota's Pine Ridge Reservation, one of the poorest Native American reservations in the United States. She was part of the Crazy Horse Clan of the Oglala Lakota (Sioux), one of the seven subtribes of the Lakota people who, along with the Dakota, make up the Great Sioux Nation. The level of poverty she experienced was unimaginable to most people.

When she lived with her grandmother and four siblings, Meals on Wheels delivered a single meal a day. Her grandmother would select one item from the small aluminum tray for herself, and the children would divide the rest. That was their meal for the day. Jovannah was so hungry that she would pick and eat grass from the yard in an attempt to make the hunger pains go away. But that was just part of what she suffered.

Beginning at the age of eight, she endured sexual abuse for years. One of her stepdads molested her for two years, and Jovannah was afraid her mother would be mad at her for not saying anything or for pretending to be asleep when it happened.

When an older cousin raped her, Jovannah tried to make him stop. "You're hurting me!" she told him.

"I'm getting you ready to be an adult," the cousin said.

Being an adult hurts, Jovannah reasoned. In her mind, that hurt was just something you had to deal with. It was something that simply happened, and it would happen all through your life. People would hurt you. They would use your body for themselves for the rest of your life. That was the way things would be, and you just had to deal with it.

At the age of fourteen, she heard about Holbrook Indian School (HIS), a boarding academy for Native American youth, grades one through twelve. Native

The Holbrook Indian School, operated by the Pacific Union Conference of the Seventh-day Adventist Church, is located in Holbrook, Arizona.

Americans are wary of Christian boarding schools, for good reason. Historically, the motto of Christian boarding schools in America was "Kill the Indian. Save the man." But the goal of HIS, Jovannah learned, was to support students on the path of healing and restoration. Holbrook was not about killing the Indian, not about killing what is Native in its students. It was about healing them and helping them to claim their identity, their culture, and their faith.

She decided HIS might be her chance for a way out. She hitched a ride in the back of a pickup truck and made the long journey to Holbrook, Arizona.

One of the first things that amazed her was the fact that the school served three meals every day. *Who eats three meals a day?* she thought. *That is something you only see on television!* Holbrook quickly became her sanctuary. It was the first time in her life she could remember not being afraid to go to sleep at night.

While at Holbrook, Jovannah was inspired to go to college, but to do so, she had to get good grades. She was getting As in all of her classes except Bible. Someone suggested that she join a Bible study group to help bring up her grade, but Jovannah had no interest in the Christian religion. In fact, she had been taught to hate it. For her, as for many Native Americans, Christianity was something to distrust. Most of the damage done to indigenous people throughout North America had been done in the name of Christianity.

She thought she could fake her way through, but as she learned about Jesus, her heart began to change. "I rejected Christianity for what I thought it stood for and accepted it for what I learned it truly stood for," she said when she was baptized at HIS.

Jovannah went on to Union College to earn her degree in education. While at Union, she met and married Zak Adams, also a graduate of Union. She knew she wanted to work with Native American communities and that HIS was the place she wanted to do it because it was a safe place. Together they returned to Holbrook, where Jovannah became vice principal and Zak a teacher.

Through programs, such as the NEW (Nutrition, Exercise, Wellness) You Health Initiative, Jovannah, Zak, and the HIS staff seek to minister to the whole person by teaching students how to improve every dimension of their lives. The program has four pillars: spiritual, mental, physical, and academic. Each pillar is a fundamental component of a student's environment and education with specific, practical applications, and each pillar empowers HIS students to establish healthy habits for a lifetime. Students are equipped to prevent mental health issues and lifestyle diseases that are present at disproportionately higher percentages in Native American populations than the national averages.

On the reservation, Native Americans live in a nation within a nation. There is a constant dissonance between the identities and value systems of those two nations. In their world, it is reported that one in three women are raped or suffer sexual abuse, almost half the population never graduates from high school, and only eight out of one hundred have college degrees. More than 50 percent of the population live at or below the poverty line, and 40 percent of those who die by suicide are between the ages of fifteen and twenty-four. (Among young adults who are eighteen to twenty-four years old, Native Americans have higher rates of suicide than the general population.) They are told, "You just have to get used to it." Or "It's just the way it is."

It is no wonder, then, that youth come to HIS with unimaginable challenges. Post-traumatic stress disorder (PTSD), substance abuse, and trust and abandonment issues seem to be the norm. At home, some students don't have electricity or running water, and they use outhouses. Every new school year at HIS, at least one student won't use the restroom because they're afraid of the toilet. Learning and functioning in an academic setting with these kinds of problems presents a unique challenge of its own.

Breaking the cycle, as Jovannah says, isn't a clean cut; it's a process. She still struggles with the painful memories of her past but talks openly with the girls she ministers to in hopes of encouraging them to receive the help and healing offered at Holbrook. Every time she courageously shares her journey from darkness into light, she slices the fabric a little deeper, helping to separate what is from what should be and introducing her students not only to the light but also to the Light of the World.

Just the Beginning

La Sierra University Center for Near Eastern Archaeology

The boy was only eight years old, but the Jordanian village elders insisted that he needed to work with the American team of archaeologists who were excavating at Tall Hisban (Heshbon), not far from Amman, Jordan. The team's purpose was to provide important information about Old Testament history, especially the time of Joshua and of Sihon, king of the Amorites who lived in Heshbon. They were searching for Bible connections with Heshbon and Sihon and the Amorites.

"We don't hire children," Larry Geraty responded. It was the summer of 1968, the first excavation season. Geraty was a doctoral student at Harvard, serving as a square supervisor at Hisban under the direction of eminent archaeologist Siegfried Horn. A square supervisor was an archaeologist responsible for a "square." Squares were usually six meters by six meters, and the people working each square consisted primarily of a square supervisor, a couple of volunteers, and a local worker or two.

The boy's father, a workman for Geraty at the site, had died suddenly of a heart attack. According to Muslim custom, he had been buried the same day. Mr. al-Barari left behind a widow, three young daughters, and a son, Mustafa. And though he was just eight, Mustafa, the elders declared, needed to provide for the family. Reluctantly, Geraty and Horn decided to give the boy a chance.

Geraty was amazed when Mustafa went to work in his dad's place that very day, right after his father was buried. Each subsequent day he faithfully showed up. He never missed a day, and he never wanted to take breaks. Sweating under the hot sun, he was eager to do anything that needed to be done. He worked harder than any two grown men.

The dig lasted five seasons, plus a short season in 1978 to excavate a church at the site. Each dig season until excavation at Hisban concluded, Mustafa al-Barari went to work. Perhaps something about the hard work of those summers early in his life motivated him for success as he matured. His small village, Hisban, did not have a high school, so he walked fifteen miles (twenty-four kilometers) roundtrip each day to attend the nearest high school, located in the city of Madaba. It took him two and a half hours each way. The boy carried his books and walked and read at the same time.

At night in their one-room house, he shared with his mother and sisters what he had learned. Mustafa trusted God, Allah, that something would change for the better. His hard work paid off. When he took the national exam at the end of high school, he earned the highest score in the entire region.

Mustafa wanted to become a physician or possibly an engineer. When he enrolled at the University of Jordan, though—having turned down a scholarship to Russia or Syria so that he could remain close to his family—the only college open to him was the business school. He enrolled in Accounting 101 with a tough professor who, after a major exam, angrily tore into the class.

"Only one student has passed," the professor declared. There was a long, anticipatory pause. "Mustafa." Later, Mustafa went to the professor's office, and he advised him to complete accounting.

Three years later, Mustafa had finished the four years of university and graduated with distinction. As the top student in the university, he had the privilege of meeting His Majesty King Hussein of Jordan, who presented him with a gold watch, a possession Mustafa would treasure for years.

Before graduation, Mustafa decided to learn more about his Islamic faith. When he enrolled in a difficult class with students studying to be imams, the professor said to him, "You have no mustache, and you're wearing jeans. Why are you coming here?" True to form, Mustafa earned the highest grade in the class.

He may have had a special motivation. At the end of the course, the professor said, "Mustafa, you've done an outstanding job in my class. What can I do for you?"

"I want to marry your daughter," Mustafa replied. Doha was a very bright student at the university. Her father agreed, and now, decades later, Mustafa and Doha have six daughters and two sons, ranging in age from twelve to twenty-five.

Pursuing a business career was obviously a good choice for Mustafa. Right out of university, he joined Deloitte & Touche in Amman, then took an even more lucrative position in Saudi Arabia. While Mustafa was working there, the prime minister of Jordan asked him to become the director of the financial and administrative affairs of a new duty-free zone in Aqaba, Jordan's only seaport. At first Mustafa declined because the government position would offer a lower salary. Then he remembered Allah and how as a boy he had walked to school and dreamed of having twenty dinars in his hand. So, he accepted.

The new endeavor proved successful. But Mustafa continued to dream. He had earned a master's degree in accounting in Jordan. Now he wanted to pass the American CPA (certified public accountant) exam. He flew to Detroit and intended to enroll in a preparatory course, but the cost was too high. So he checked into an inexpensive motel and holed up with review books. He passed all sections of the CPA exam on his first try, a success achieved by few CPA students.

Mustafa decided he wanted to earn an MBA (master of business administration). That fall, he left his family with his in-laws in Amman and moved into Sierra Towers at La Sierra University to pursue the degree.

A little over a year later, degree in hand, Mustafa started a doctoral program in England. Just a few months into it, however, the Jordanian prime minister called him to be director general of the country's Audit Bureau. Half a year later, he was promoted to president of the bureau. "The government can't spend a dinar without my approval," he told Geraty, with whom he was still in contact. By this time, his circle of acquaintances included treasury secretaries of numerous nations.

In a region where corruption is a major problem, Mustafa was determined that Jordan's finances would be grounded in transparency and integrity. When he discovered that someone in government was spending in violation of the law, Mustafa challenged him. In the resulting power struggle, it was Mustafa who was fired. He would not back down from the values he had developed in his life that were reinforced at La Sierra's School of Business.

Just days later, Mustafa received a letter from His Majesty King Abdullah II of Jordan. "Consider yourself as on vacation," the letter said. Not long after, a new government was elected. As one of his first official acts, the new prime minister reinstated Mustafa as president of the Audit Bureau.

After several years, Mustafa returned to the private sector, serving on corporate boards and working as a consultant for the potash industry, the largest natural resource in Jordan. The move left him with time to visit with his family, help charities, and volunteer in his community. He also became the president of Friends of Hisban.

During the most recent government shake-up, however, His Majesty King Abdullah II of Jordan appointed Mustafa to Jordan's Senate, where he assists the government as a financial specialist and travels the world representing his country on behalf of his king.

It all began a half-century ago when a little boy who had just buried his father picked up a basket and went to work for an Adventist team of archaeologists who taught him valuable life lessons. And that was just the beginning.

The Ripple Effect

Zoz Amba Foundation

Shashe Kassaw was born in northwest Ethiopia in the small village of Ababikla. Her parents were illiterate peasant farmers. They saw no value in educating their children. Instead, they intended to give their daughters in marriage as early as possible. The average age of girls given in marriage in their country was twelve. Little Shashe dreaded the day she turned twelve.

Her parents may not have had education in mind for her, but Shashe had her own ideas. She dreamed of going to school. When she asked her parents if she could go to the small elementary school not far from her village, her parents said no. Shashe was determined. She desperately wanted to join the lucky few in school. She begged, she pleaded, she cajoled, but her parents would not budge.

Time marched on. Her older sister turned twelve and was given in marriage. Shashe knew her turn was coming. When the dreaded day finally arrived, Shashe's parents informed her that she would soon be getting married.

"We have given our word to the parents of your future husband," they said. Shashe knew her fate was sealed.

But she wasn't going to go down without a fight. She pleaded with her parents to please spare her. "Send me to school instead," she begged. But her plea fell on deaf ears. They refused to relent.

Mustering all her courage, Shashe informed her parents that she would take drastic measures to make sure that the marriage failed. "I will do this," she promised.

Her parents knew their daughter was not bluffing. She was very determined and decisive. So, they backed off, temporarily.

When she turned thirteen, they tricked her into going to visit family members in the next village. Shashe did not suspect that what she most dreaded was awaiting her there. When she and her parents reached the village, the drumbeats started, and the wedding songs erupted. She knew then that what she tried hard to avoid had now become unavoidable. She was angry, very angry! Her parents literally grabbed her, dressed her up, and wedded her to a total stranger.

She was taken away kicking and screaming and began planning her escape immediately. She ran away from her husband soon after the wedding and returned home. Her parents beat her severely and returned her to her new husband. She ran away again. Shashe was prepared for a long fight, and she was determined to win it. She kept running away, and they kept beating her and returning her to her husband.

It was time to take a more drastic measure. One day, she picked up a rope and ran away. She made sure that people saw her with a rope to make them think that she was running away to hang herself. The news of her disappearance spread fast and wide, and her parents were panic-stricken. They knew what their daughter was capable of doing when sufficiently provoked.

An intense search ensued, but Shashe was nowhere to be found. She hid herself well in a thick forest and waited it out. She could hear the search party going back and forth and calling her name. In desperation, her father blurted out a promise that was music to her ears. He said, "We promise that we will end the marriage and send you to school. Please come back to us. Don't hurt yourself. We will keep our promise."

Hearing that, she came out of hiding and triumphantly presented herself to a stunned and relieved search party. Her parents kept their promise, and Shashe graduated from high school in 2014. She is now a senior chemistry major at Gondar University in northwest Ethiopia. Her last grade report had a cumulative GPA (grade point average) of 3.87, a remarkable achievement for a country girl.

Shashe's goal is to convince rural peasant parents that educating their daught-ers will pay dividends. She also wants to inspire rural girls and their mothers with the fact that there is a better alternative in life than early marriage. Shashe's mother and grandmother were her worst roadblocks, and she is determined to change minds, touting her success in school and her career as a professional woman.

The school Shashe attended, Worku Jember High School, was built by the Zoz Amba Foundation, founded by Adugnaw Worku, an Ethiopian native who had the opportunity to pursue his dream of education and had a passion to return to his native country and help his people as he was helped. The Zoz Amba Foundation's goal is to partner with community leaders, faith groups, local government agencies, and NGOs (nongovernmental organizations) to support sustainable community development in rural Ethiopia, with special emphasis on issues impacting women and girls. They strive to empower women and girls in rural Ethiopia by eradicating female circumcision, early marriage, and illiteracy and by providing access to clean water, flour mills, and training on basic health and hygiene.

Worku Jember High School has been the best-equipped school in the area, thanks to qualified teachers, free faculty and staff housing, a reliable and sustainable solar energy source, access to clean water, restrooms, a computer lab, a library, science lab facilities, classrooms, a health center, and administrative and office spaces.

The Zoz Amba Foundation seeks to empower women in other practical ways as well, such as providing flour mills for grinding grain. In traditional Ethiopian culture, women are responsible for all household chores, including cooking for the family and grinding grain. Grains are a significant share of Ethiopian food staples. For thousands of years, women have been grinding their grain between two stones, often with a baby on their back. It takes a considerable amount of time to grind enough grain for the day. In addition, it is hard work and physically exhausting. Stone grit accompanies this method of making flour and erodes teeth, causing dental problems and decay.*

The Zoz Amba Foundation established flour mills. The time saved between grinding grains using primitive stone grinders and using modern flour mills is astronomical. Now, women with access to a modern flour mill in their neighborhood have more time for other chores, and girls have more time to study. Each flour mill serves approximately eight thousand people, and women and girls are the clear beneficiaries.

In addition to the flour mills, the Zoz Amba Foundation conducts women's health and hygiene projects, which have been enormously popular and successful. In rural Ethiopia, the culture doesn't talk about menstruation. It just happens, to the surprise of girls going through puberty. The goal is for girls to understand that menstruation is perfectly natural and necessary for child-bearing.

The women and girls are trained to make their own feminine pads out of local materials, and some young women have been trained to make pads using sewing machines. They have been given new sewing machines and start-up money to serve their respective communities by making and selling the pads. Parents, religious leaders, and young people have all been educated about the harmful effects of genital cutting, early marriage, illiteracy, and lack of basic health and hygiene. School absenteeism by teenage girls has been wiped out in the schools where such training and pad-making has occurred. Extensive media coverage has helped to get the word out to other communities so that they, too, can help themselves.

Through tiny ripples, the Zoz Amba Foundation is effecting major change in rural Ethiopia, one person, one project, one student at a time, liberating and empowering girls and women through education.

---

* "Projects," Zoz Amba Foundation, 2017, http://adugnawworku.com/zozamba/projects.html.

Courageous Compassion

Holbrook Indian School

Adrian Wiles was seven years old when his older brother taught him how to drink alcohol and use drugs. At the time, he didn't think anything was wrong with his life; it was all he knew. And it was a hard life. He didn't know his father, and his mother drank a lot. Sometimes she accidentally locked him out of the house, and he had to sleep outside. Because he was scared and cold, Adrian would crawl under the porch and sleep with the dogs.

He began to get into a lot of trouble. Some of his uncles and aunts had gone to Holbrook Indian School (HIS) in the past, and they encouraged his mother to enroll him.

"It will be better for him," they said.

Native Americans are naturally wary of boarding schools because of the forced assimilation they were subjected to in the late nineteenth through mid-twentieth centuries. In an effort to westernize Native Americans, the government forced children to attend in the belief that with education, they would merge peacefully into the growing European-American culture. Although many of the schools were run by religious organizations, children were often treated harshly, suffering all manner of abuse, and many died.

HIS was established as a mission school for the unreached Native Americans, but unlike its predecessors, HIS wanted to restore the image of the Creator in their students by promoting the development of the whole person. In that way, they knew the healing process could begin. Students would then become free to explore a personal relationship with Christ and a healthy relationship with others. This is particularly important because most of the students who attend HIS are not Seventh-day Adventists and haven't heard the gospel message. They come from various backgrounds and face similar negative circumstances.

On Adrian's first night in the dorm, his mother put him in bed and sat with him until he began to fall asleep. When she left the room, Adrian woke up and jumped out of bed, running after her. He caught up with her in the hallway and grabbed her by the legs, crying. He begged her not to leave him.

"Go back to your room," his mother told him, "and stop being such a big, old baby."

Crying, Adrian refused to let her go. Finally, his cousins picked him up and carried him back to his room. As he looked out the window and saw his mother drive away, he cried even harder. His cousins didn't feel sorry for him. He was creating a scene, and they didn't like that. They told him to stop crying.

But he couldn't. He cried every night for a month. He missed his family even though they were mean to him. He had a difficult time adjusting to how the teachers and students treated him. They were friendly and kind. Adrian didn't know what to make of people being nice to him. It wasn't what he was used to.

After he had been at HIS for a few weeks, the school chaplain asked him and another student to lead worship. Adrian was nervous about standing in front of the other students, but he got up and spoke about his home life. When he finished speaking, he felt a lot better about being at the school. Other students shared their experiences, and they were similar. From that moment on, Adrian didn't feel so alone.

Although he was in the third grade when he arrived at HIS, Adrian couldn't read. One of his teachers inspired him with the desire to learn and taught him how to read. He also learned about hygiene and how to take care of himself.

Each year, as he returned to HIS, Adrian learned more about who God was, and he learned how to pray. What he learned about God led him to the decision to stop drinking and using drugs. Then, in seventh grade, he made the decision to be baptized. His mother and brothers made fun of him for becoming a Christian. They teased him about refusing to eat pork and other unclean meat. They couldn't understand why he kept offering to help with chores around the house. But slowly, in time, they began to realize that Adrian was sincere in his new beliefs and that he had really changed.

One day his mother said to him, "We are glad that you are changing, and that you are getting an education." Her words filled him with happiness.

The summer before his senior year, Adrian prayed all summer long that his cousins who were in the first through ninth grades would be able to attend HIS. He was thrilled when God answered his prayer, and his cousins joined him at school that year.

His youngest cousin, Josiah, was in the first grade, and like Adrian, Josiah wasn't happy when he arrived. On his first night in the dorm, he cried and cried, asking to return home. Adrian was able to do something that no one had done for him on his first night. He went to his little cousin's room to comfort him.

"Try not to think about it," Adrian told him. "I was in your spot when I was small. You'll get used to it. It will be OK."

One of the aspects of HIS that makes it unique is the size of the student body. It is small enough that it feels like a family. The older children mentor the younger ones, reading them stories, worshiping with them, praying together, and helping them do laundry. Girls become sisters, and the boys become brothers. The ratio of staff to student is nearly two to one, so there is plenty of opportunity for the staff to help the older kids learn to be good mentors. The size also makes it almost impossible for a student to fall through the cracks.

In time, Josiah grew to really love HIS. He is very happy there now, partly because Adrian took the time to share compassion with him.

After graduation, Adrian plans to go to college. He doesn't like to think about where he would be if it hadn't been for HIS, but he suspects he would still be using drugs and alcohol to numb the pain of the life he was born into. Instead, at HIS, Adrian found that he has a heavenly Father who will never leave him, and he's learned that his life has meaning and purpose.

Adrian in back, with Quentin, Skyler, Corwin, and Adrienna

*"Blessed are those who hunger
and thirst for righteousness,
for they will be filled."*

—Matthew 5:6, NIV

Go Healthy for Good

Hope Channel

Susan had several health challenges. Like many people, she was overweight; in August 2012, she was diagnosed with prediabetes. Just a month later, God led her to a show on the Hope Channel, *Go Healthy for Good*. She watched in amazement as host Dr. Nerida McKibben, a physician with experience in lifestyle medicine, explained how simple lifestyle changes could drastically improve her health.

Susan had decided that she didn't want to go on medication to treat her condition. Her doctor had advised that she eat no more than fifteen grams of carbohydrates, but she was confused about the difference between simple and complex carbohydrates. Clearly and methodically, Dr. Nerida explained the differences and offered helpful advice.

Things began to change for Susan. Putting into practice the positive lifestyle changes she had learned, she lost thirty-six pounds, reversed her prediabetes, and lowered her blood pressure without medication. In addition, her heartbeat was strong, and her joints were pain-free. Eager to share the positive changes in her life, Susan posted her experience on the *Go Healthy for Good* Facebook page.

Dr. Nerida saw Susan's story and phoned her to see whether there was anything else Hope Channel could do.

Susan was surprised and delighted. "I have more questions about things in the Bible," she responded. "I'd love to study the Bible regularly with someone."

Dr. Nerida immediately set up phone appointments to study God's Word with Susan every weekend. Susan now has a new life, one with Jesus in control, a healthy lifestyle, and a supportive, encouraging church community. Dr. Nerida continues to connect with Susan and encourage her to keep up the positive lifestyle changes.

Go Healthy for Good, the program that changed Susan's life so remarkably, is an hour-long, live, interactive television program focusing on health and wellness. It was designed to help the average person who is confused by contradicting information on health and wellness to navigate the science from constantly changing media reports. Though it was designed for people with questions about common

Go Healthy for Good

Susan found *Go Healthy for Good* on the Hope Channel and, as a result, turned her life and health around.

problems, such as family issues or stress, it also engages those who are interested in wholistic health or want to take positive action toward wellness but don't know where to find answers. Dr. Nerida, a New Zealand-born obstetrician and gynecological surgeon who is passionate about enabling people to achieve their greatest health potential, acts as host, analyzing and explaining healthy options and choices.

Wanting everyone to live life to the fullest, she integrates wholistic principles into medical treatments and procedures. Dr. Nerida knows firsthand the incredible power unleashed when her patients make healthy lifestyle choices. Viewers can watch people from many walks of life make wiser decisions and see their lives transformed. They can learn from the experience of others how to make positive changes in their health and never look back. Viewers submit questions, and Dr. Nerida and her guest experts answer them live on the show.

Dr. Nerida believes that the world is in the midst of a health revolution, with many varied theories on how to achieve good health. In the midst of this confusion, the mission of *Go Healthy for Good* is to present balanced, consistent, and practical advice that is backed by research and the Bible.

She is always excited to hear from regular viewers who have incorporated that advice in their lives. They tell about reversing their lifestyle-related diseases such as diabetes, obesity, high cholesterol, and high blood pressure as well as simply being motivated to take better care of themselves. With social media, it is possible to maintain supportive relationships with viewers for months, or in some cases, years, encouraging them to never give up. When Dr. Nerida meets viewers in person, they typically express how much they enjoy the exercise, cooking, or comedy segments.

Taking the latest research in lifestyle medicine and conveying it to the viewers in positive, intelligible, and creative ways remains interesting and fun. Dr. Nerida is grateful to God for the opportunity to be part of *Go Healthy for Good* and to impact the lives of people like Susan and Christine, who come to the show looking for answers about topics such as psoriasis and type 2 diabetes.

"I watched your show about psoriasis and learned so much I didn't know," Christine told Dr. Nerida. "I have had psoriasis for about five or six years and type 2 diabetes for eighteen. My diabetes is under control after losing a hundred and thirty pounds with God's help, so I don't take medication. I just test my blood sugar each day. Both psoriasis and type 2 diabetes run in my family. I can't thank you enough for doing shows on these subjects.

"I believe God deserves all the glory and praise for leading me to your show where I could learn this information. I had been having tremors localized to my hands, legs, and feet. I asked my pastor if it were possible to be anointed for healing. It was arranged, and I met with the pastor, head deacon, and my husband on a Sabbath after the service was over. That was about five years ago, and I still occasionally have the tremors, but God has done so many powerful things in my life!"

Because of what she learned on *Go Healthy for Good*, Christine no longer takes medication for her type 2 diabetes. She still has a few more pounds to lose, but she is determined to maintain a healthy lifestyle. Dr. Nerida connected her with a local lifestyle medicine physician and hopes to see Christine's health improve even further.

Dr. Nerida has witnessed many miracles such as these when God's simple remedies are learned and applied. Vitality is restored, health regained, disease reversed, and hope revived. Many people needlessly suffer from lifestyle-related diseases because they do not know what is causing their problems. *Go Healthy for Good* provides an avenue to change all that.

The program airs on Hope Channel, a Christian television network with fifty channels around the world, broadcasting in fifty-seven languages. The mission of Hope Channel is to share God's good news for a better life today and for eternity. Their programs focus on faith, health, relationships, and community. Programs on each channel are contextualized for the local culture and are broadcast in many languages. With every episode of *Go Healthy for Good*, Hope Channel is beaming a message of health and wellness into the homes of millions around the world.

Call to Action

Good News TV

Vicki Montano grew up knowing she was part Jewish; her mother's family had a rabbi or two as great-grandparents. Her family even attended synagogue sometimes and occasionally celebrated Passover with extended family. When she was a junior in high school, she had also attended a Protestant church for about a year with a friend and again after her first marriage.

Then an injury left her sidelined at home for six weeks. While flipping through the channels looking for something to stave off boredom, she discovered Good News TV. The channel aired 24/7 with thought-provoking, Christ-centered programs designed to nurture and encourage a deep personal relationship with God and issue a call to grow and walk with Him through Christian service.

Enthralled, Vicki first learned about the character of God. Then she learned about the Sabbath and the Protestant Reformation. She was amazed and felt as though a light had gone on as she watched. Suddenly all the history classes she'd had in school began to snap into focus. She finally understood why history flowed the way it did, beginning with the history of the Jews, the role of Rome, and the difference between Christians and Catholics. Eventually, she even began to understand Bible prophecy. For the first time, she was able to take all that fragmented information and see the dynamic that tied it all together. Once she understood the spiritual war underlying history, it all made sense.

She was excited about all she was learning about the character of Christ and the history and ongoing influence of the spiritual war in which the earth was embroiled. She felt the insights were valuable additions to her life. They gave her the strong foundation she needed to answer the question, Why am I here? She was gratified to realize she is part of God's awesome plan. It is larger than she is but also personal to her.

Vicki realized that she was still just watching TV; she wasn't engaged. One day as she watched she saw an appeal by Luke and Susan Skelton, the managing director of Good News TV and his wife, to join the group at a camp meeting, and she was impressed to get involved.

Her first attempt at getting to church didn't work because she couldn't find

Vicki Montano (right) encountered Good News TV while recovering from an injury. She was excited with what she learned, developed a relationship with Jesus, and began volunteering with the GNTV ministry team (above).

anything to wear that seemed appropriate in the 120-degree heat. But the next week she got it together and made her way to Camelback Seventh-day Adventist Church. She spotted Susan at the church but was too shy to say anything. Susan was busy anyway, so Vicki returned home, still feeling pretty pleased with her adventure. As she was settling in to her Sabbath, there was a knock at the door. She was surprised to find Vera Onkoba and her brother, who were ambassadors for Good News TV—church members in a broadcasting area who visit viewers, build relations, and mentor people as they start attending church. They were standing on her doorstep with a book that she had requested from Good News TV as a free offer.

Vicki was amazed. She invited them in, and they visited. As she received the book, she had another surprise waiting for her. Vera had brought her *The Great Controversy*. She hadn't realized when she requested it that the book was by Ellen White, an author with whom she was familiar. Her grandmother had left Vicki her Bible and a book: a 1975 edition of *The Desire of Ages*, also by Ellen White. Vicki had read chapters of *The Desire of Ages* and had loved the book. She truly believed the reverence for Christ in that book matched and resonated with the reverence and insight of the teaching she found on Good News TV and that one of the reasons she had responded so strongly to the programming was because of her exposure to that book.

She discovered that each avenue to lead someone to Christ was important. The literature ministry and the local television ministry supported and fed each other, and together they worked to bring people out of their homes and into the churches. In time, Vicki became involved with Good News TV and the church video ministry as a volunteer, though she had never considered herself someone who joined clubs.

Today she is amazed that a simple television program could lead to such huge changes in her life, changes she feels are important and healthy. In addition to the spiritual changes, Vicki has experienced other changes that have dramatically impacted her life. She became committed to a vegan lifestyle, which resulted in improved physical health with reduced food-related problems and seasonal allergies and a stable, healthy weight. She developed goals to improve her physical and spiritual life, and now she has the support to achieve those goals. Her new, wholesome avenues for social interaction replaced going to clubs and drinking parties. She has developed more conviction to say no to bad choices and unhealthy relationships and begun to truly understand that those bad choices lead to an erosion of quality of life.

The local ministry was vital to introducing Vicki to those important truths but also critical in helping her to *stay* in the influence and lifestyle of the message she had embraced. Initially, she had been drawn intellectually to the teaching. Once she understood something mentally, she knew it was easy for her to simply move on to the next topic. She could have watched the program and checked off the line item of "religious stuff to know" before moving on to sci-fi movies or learning Spanish. It was the invitation, Vicki knew, that had made the difference. That was what had pulled her off the couch and into the church.

That simple invitation to the camp meeting had changed her life. Because of it, she had felt welcomed and empowered to take the next step—to become involved personally in the truth—a step she had never taken before in any other spiritual encounters. She had been stirred by the literature before, but until Good News TV, she hadn't been called to action. With her answer, she looks forward to many years of maintaining and improving her spiritual experience.

New Challenges, New Opportunities

Cuba Adventist Theological Seminary

Dr. Annia Vives and her husband shared a dream that, eventually, he would be able to study to become a pastor. Two years after their marriage, he was accepted into the ministerial program at Cuba Adventist Theological Seminary. They moved to Havana with their one-year-old daughter and moved in with her parents, who were ill, and her younger sister, who used a wheelchair because a brain tumor caused paralysis on her right side. The home wasn't very close to the seminary, so Annia's husband wasn't often home.

Despite the severe economic crisis in Cuba during the 1990s, God helped the little family overcome every challenge that surfaced. Annia worked as a physician, which was the sole means of financial support for her family and the only way to finance her husband's studies. At that time, the monthly salary for a recently graduated physician was 231 Cuban pesos (CUP), roughly equivalent to US$13. A pound of rice could cost as much as CUP$100. Annia can't explain it, but God always seemed to multiply their resources just enough to meet their needs.

Annia visited the seminary a couple of times, and she was very impressed by the place. It was charming and warm, and a Christian spirit permeated the campus. She thirsted for knowledge of the Bible and for ways to connect deeply with her patients and other people. That desire overflowed as she listened to her husband's stories during the times when he visited their home.

During his third year, Annia's husband received an offer to work at a church near the school while he continued with his studies. It was truly a challenge to move their little family to a city where they didn't know a single person, to find a new job for Annia so that she could help support the family while he studied, and to take care of their young daughter, who at that time was three years old. In addition, she helped in the church, which met in the living room of their house.

Each trial they faced brought with it a reward. The experience of working with the church motivated Annia to begin studying theology along with her husband. However, she was not able to quit working because her job was the only family income. God answered their prayers; her work granted permission to attend classes in the mornings and work in the afternoons. She consulted with

New Challenges, New Opportunities

her patients during their appointments and then afterward visited many of them in their homes. She changed her on-call schedule to Sundays from eight o'clock in the morning to eight o'clock in the evening. It was a grueling schedule, but she survived with the help of her husband, the seminary faculty, and church members.

Annia enjoyed her classes, even the tests, and relished the opportunity to prove that seminary was the best place for her to prepare to be the partner her pastor-husband needed.

The new semester of classes was already in session when Annia realized she was pregnant. It was a high-risk pregnancy, but she continued to study and work until one month before giving birth to her second child. When their baby was three months old, Annia went back to class. She sat at the back to nurse the baby, and life seemed full because of her love for her baby and the joy of studying.

The support of her teachers and colleagues led her to love the school more and more every day. She felt like part of a great family, and her work as a physician was enriched as a result. It allowed her to testify to her patients about what God was continually doing in her life. Additionally, her studies trained her how to respond to her colleagues' theological questions.

When Cuba Adventist Theological Seminary received accreditation by the Accrediting Association of Seventh-day Adventist Schools, which allowed it to be a graduate school under the sponsorship of the Inter-American Adventist Theological Seminary, one of Annia's professors suggested that she begin a master's program since she had all the academic prerequisites to do so. As always, Annia and her husband took the matter to God in prayer. God's answer was clear, and she began to study at the graduate level.

Over the course of four summers, Annia continued working as a physician and attending classes in the mornings. Every day, God's Word gave her the courage she needed to continue. Some questioned why a woman would go to the trouble of studying for a master's in pastoral theology when there were so many roadblocks to putting it to use. God's answer was far too convincing for her to become discouraged.

After four years of intense sacrifices, Annia became the first woman in Cuba to graduate with a master's degree in pastoral theology through the Inter-American Adventist Theological Seminary and only the second in the whole Inter-American Division of Seventh-day Adventists.

During her second course in graduate school, the seminary staff asked her to teach the Healthy Lifestyle class, a subject related to her medical profession. She accepted without hesitation. Annia is currently a professor at the Cuba Adventist Theological Seminary and the director of the Department of Research and Publications. She is proof that there is no better place to work than where God has called.

Sola Scriptura

Good News TV

There was no Christian teaching or church in Brian Shamrock's family, but he had read some of the Bible on his own. He had heard about Jesus, but all he really knew was that he shouldn't say His name or he'd get slapped. While visiting a Baptist church as a young teen, he responded to an altar call and was baptized soon afterward. He attended church faithfully every Sunday morning, Sunday night, and Wednesday night for a couple of years.

The church's sermons and lessons were mostly nebulous platitudes about grace or faith. Members spent most of their time playing games. The meetings felt more like babysitting than Bible study.

One time, Brian shared some sin struggles with the youth group leader in private.

"You really need to stop sinning," the youth group leader told him. "The Holy Spirit leaves you when you sin. You need to clean up your act." Brian decided he couldn't be good enough to be a Christian, so he started looking for a god that he could worship.

Over the next twelve years, Brian studied and practiced the occult with a focus on Wicca (pagan witchcraft), Druidism, and later Kabbalah, trying to find a god that would accept him. He was in college in his late twenties when a fellow student invited him to the Church of Christ. He attended there for about three years and experienced some good growth and learning.

Then he graduated and left the state, a convenient excuse to stop meeting for regular fellowship. In reality, he left because of confusion and doubts about his salvation as well as personal issues that were mounting due to disobedience and rebellion. The next eight years were a spiral of darkness.

On Father's Day in 2009, Brian crashed his Harley and spent a week in the ICU (intensive care unit). After a few days, the surgeon came to see him.

"Brian, you are what we call around here a mini miracle."

"What do you mean?" Brian asked.

"Well," the surgeon told him, "as we were preparing to do emergency surgery to put your skull back together, we were looking down at your exposed brain. I was just getting ready to dive in when the other surgeon grabbed my hand. We watched in amazement as, in about ninety seconds, all of the little fingers and joints of your fractured skull folded back together like a hand and glove. They closed up over your brain all by themselves. You have to understand that only one in ten thousand skulls will do that, but yours went back together as good as, if not better than, we ever could have done it. All we had to do was sew you up. Someone up there loves you!"

"Amen for that," Brian replied.

Because his injuries were severe, Brian spent six months recovering, but what should have been the worst day of his life turned out to be the biggest blessing because it became the catalyst that brought him closer to God. When he was feeling better, he decided to go to some bars to find some female companionship. But as the thought entered his mind, a deep sorrow washed over him, worse than any depressive episode of his past.

On his knees, he cried out to God, "If there is more to life than this, please reveal it to me!"

The response he heard was, "Brian, you've known Me for twenty-five years. Why don't you just try it My way?"

Brian knew God was speaking to him. Almost in spite of himself, he began to grow and learn new truths, such as that the Holy Spirit had claimed him for God, that God wasn't waiting for him to get "good enough" to come to Him, that faith was increased by hearing the Word. He learned that we are called to persevere through trials. He began devouring the Word and fellowshiping with Jesus.

But Brian also experienced a great deal of false teaching and was sometimes told "Keep quiet" or "You talk too much" when he pointed out something from Scripture that didn't match what the church was teaching. Confused and frustrated, he prayed, "God, I thought I was doing what you wanted me to do!"

He began to get involved more deeply in his church, helping to facilitate Sunday School class, teaching kids on Wednesdays, and playing guitar every Sunday morning in front of a couple hundred people. He was happier than he ever thought he could be, until one Monday morning when he got a call from the pastor.

"What you said about the rapture at Sunday School yesterday is not what our church teaches," the pastor informed him.

The group had been studying 2 Thessalonians, and they were discussing the differences between post-tribulation, mid-tribulation, and pre-tribulation raptures. Brian also disagreed with his church's view on the topic of hell. Unlike what they were suggesting, he found that the Bible taught that hellfire results in the destruction of body and soul instead of eternal torture. He had heard a lot about how we are justified by Christ alone but rarely about Christ then calling us to follow Him in the process of sanctification, maturing in faith, overcoming sin, and becoming more Christlike. What he did hear many times was that when the rebuilding of the physical temple in Jerusalem began, it would mark the beginning of the tribulation. But that was dangerous because people wouldn't "get their act together" until after that happened. He couldn't reconcile those theological concepts with Scripture, so he began to doubt whether he should be at church.

He cried out to God and fully surrendered, telling Him, "I am willing to do whatever you tell me to do. I just want to know the truth!"

Three days later, Brian accidentally pressed channel twenty-two on his TV remote instead of twenty-one. He stumbled onto a different Christian channel called Good News TV, which he had never noticed before. Pastor Doug Batchelor was talking about the Sabbath. Over the course of the next hour, Brian was amazed that Pastor Doug talked about worship and how the Sabbath is important to God. He had never before even considered the question about which day the Sabbath was, much less whether it was important. After watching, he began his own study and prayer.

Brian studied the subject more, and over the next four days, he became convinced that the Sabbath was on Saturday rather than Sunday and that he needed to follow Jesus in *all* of His truth. He called the number on the screen and talked to the phone attendant, Susan, at Good News TV. She told him that Seventh-day Adventist churches kept the Sabbath, that there were many in Phoenix, and that he'd be welcome to attend any of them. After speaking and praying with Susan for about an hour, Brian asked whether they could meet in person at Camelback Seventh-day Adventist Church.

He started learning about the Adventist Church because he knew almost nothing about it. Again, he was amazed that people were teaching what he understood from his study of Scripture about the rapture and hell. He and his nephews started attending Camelback. They met some wonderful people and have had many opportunities to learn, grow, and serve. There is no doubt in his mind that God used Good News TV to answer his prayerful yearning for God's truth.

Miracle Water

Pine Springs Ranch

On a beautiful fall day, Gerry Chudleigh, Southeastern California Conference (SECC) youth director, invited Dennis Nutter, Pine Springs Ranch camp director, to bring his Bible and join him at Pine Springs Ranch for a day of prayer and seeking God's direction for the SECC youth department in the coming calendar year. Pine Springs Ranch is a Christian youth camp and retreat center owned and operated by the Southeastern California Conference of Seventh-day Adventists. It's located on 481 acres in the San Jacinto Mountains.

When they arrived, Gerry suggested that they separate, find a private, quiet spot, pray for each other, and then ask God to point them to a Scripture passage that would define or clarify the theme of their assigned areas of ministry. They would meet several hours later and tell each other about their time with the Lord. They would ask themselves why the Lord had pointed them to that particular passage and what principles they could apply as they worked with the young people in their conference.

The Lord directed Dennis to the story of the woman at the well in John, chapter four. He read and reread the passage and tried to figure out the principles that he could apply when he and the camp staff planned the summer's program. He liked the idea that the story took place at a well because there had been a miracle in the history of the camp about water, or the lack thereof, from the hillside lateral wells.

He pictured the young people who would be coming from a variety of backgrounds and family situations. Dennis imagined that there would be campers who weren't sure there really was a God, or, if there were, they might think He didn't have much to do with or for them. But he believed that they would be watching the staff, listening to their instructors, and learning from their counselors. He hoped the campers would conclude that there must be a God because "my counselor knows Him and speaks to Him and about Him every day." He hoped that because of the time they spent at camp, they, like the Samaritans who heard the good news from the woman at the well, would be able to say, "We no longer believe just because of what you said; now we have heard for ourselves, and we know that this man really is the Savior of the world" (John 4:42, NIV).

Based on his time with Gerry and the Lord that day, Dennis would often remind the staff that every class, program, outpost, Friday night pageant, walk-thru-the-Bible, Saturday night program, and one-on-one conversation with campers at Pine Springs Ranch should lead to decisions for Christ at the end of the campers' stay. When planning any aspect of the camp program, rather than asking, "What's wrong with *this*?" or "Why can't we *that*?" they needed to learn to ask, "How does this contribute to decisions at the end of the week?"

One Friday morning during staff worship, Dennis had to inform the staff that unless Pine Springs Ranch experienced a miracle, the camp would shut down that Sunday, just as 225 campers were scheduled to arrive for another week of summer camp. They would be joining a staff of more than 70. As Dennis explained, the twenty-eight-thousand-gallon water tank had just enough water—hopefully—to get the camp through to Sunday morning, but not enough to do so much as a load of laundry after that. Then he told the staff about the water miracle of 1970 when God provided water under similar circumstances; could it happen again?

There were a number of buildings on the site, and they all relied on the water tank, as did the campers, staff, and animals. The tank was spring-fed through a three-inch pipe and sat on the hill above the camp. The slow-flowing spring water was never enough to fill the small intake pipe, and it took at least three days to fill the tank when it was empty—and that was if no one in the camp was using water. With a full camp in session, the water would gradually diminish all week. Weeks with smaller camp groups helped the water supply by allowing the tank to refill slowly.

At the conclusion of that morning's worship, the staff members committed to a twenty-four-hour prayer marathon to begin at noon, with each person pledging to pray for fifteen or thirty minutes by signing up for designated times on a printed schedule. The plan was to petition God that if it were His will, water would be provided. In the meantime, the staff tried to conserve water.

At noon, the staff began to pray continuously. Checks throughout Friday afternoon and evening showed the water levels dropping. At lights out, the tank was almost empty. Dennis considered having water trucked in just to get the camp through to Sunday morning.

The praying continued all night long. All available staff members went to the six o'clock staff worship in the lodge Sabbath morning. During worship, camp ranger Ivan Graham rushed into the room with the news: the tank, which had been empty just hours before, was now overflowing and had water running out the top and down the hillside below the tank.

Cabin devotionals that morning were full of praise and thanksgiving. The personal testimonies of the staff and counselors around the little lakeside campfires following the Friday night pageant all gave God the credit for saving the camp.

Suddenly God became very real to the campers. In addition, campers learned that Christians can have a lot of fun, get exercise, learn new life skills, enjoy laughter, and make a positive difference in their homes, schools, and communities.

As for the water, there were no more shortages the rest of the summer.

Radio's Long Reach

Your Story Hour

Susy and Phil Downer came to the Lord on the brink of divorce. Little did they know that a ministry started by a handful of adults and college young people as a Saturday afternoon story hour group for neighborhood children would impact their children in a powerful way. In 1985, the Downers were attending a home show in Atlanta. They had three children at the time (a four-year-old, a two-year-old, and a six-month-old) and were very focused on how they could develop in their children a love for the Lord Jesus and His Word. As they walked around the corner from an aisle of garden displays, they encountered a big rack of cassettes containing stories from the worldwide, non-denominational children's radio ministry Your Story Hour.

"The ministry representative explained their goal of imparting to the listening children a love for God's Word, in addition to building about sixty positive character qualities into them," says Susy, who had recently left her job as an attorney with Delta Air Lines to be a stay-at-home mom and homeschool teacher. "My husband gasped when I said I wanted to spend almost five hundred dollars on the entire set! He ultimately agreed that this sounded like the best investment we could make in our children. We eventually added three more children to our crew, and from that day on, *Your Story Hour* was our best friend. We told Uncle Dan one time that if we had a fire, we would grab our Bibles and the big white cases of *Your Story Hour*—and of course our children!"

Before the Downer children could read, they listened to *Your Story Hour* tapes for their quiet time. When they cleaned their rooms, rode in the car, rested, or had downtime, they listened—over and over again, they listened.

"It's tragic," says Susy, "that many of our nation's children today have never heard of Hudson Taylor, Fanny Crosby, or dozens of other men and women who have had a huge impact for the Lord on countless people.

"One of the many reasons God gave us the Bible is so that we could see the mistakes others made to help us avoid them and to put godly people before us to model. *Your Story Hour* does the same. It is much easier to deal with matters of character after listening to a story about that character quality—or lack thereof.

For example, it is more effective for a child to hear a story where he lives through the ramifications of shoplifting with another child than for his dad to say, 'Shoplifting is wrong and will hurt your life.' "

Susy and Phil discovered that listening to the stories with their children made conversations about spiritual matters very natural. Letting their daughters "live" with Esther as she stepped out in faith in spite of fearing for her life had more impact than just encouraging them to "be like Esther."

Paul, their four-year-old son, listened to the whole eight-tape series "Acts of the Apostles" three times in three weeks. Driving with him in the car one day shortly afterward, Susy noticed that her son was unusually quiet.

Your Story Hour featured Aunt Sue and Uncle Dan.

"What are you thinking about, Paul?" Susy asked.

He replied quietly, "Mom, I was just thinking, if I had to face death like my namesake did, would I be strong enough in Jesus not to deny Him?"

"That is representative of the impact *Your Story Hour* has had on our children," Susy says, adding, "Paul is now a pastor."

During the years when the Downers spoke as a family at various conferences, they put out brochures for *Your Story Hour* on their book table. And whenever Susy spoke on discipling children or how to have a godly home, she always mentioned the value of having children grow up with *Your Story Hour*.

"No matter the denomination where we were speaking," she says, "I was always confident that no one would have an issue with the theology behind the stories because they are so solid biblically, and they do not deal with issues that divide denominations.

"Of course, the scriptwriters have to add details around the biblical accounts in order to tell the story. When I first started listening, periodically I would think to myself, 'Hmmm. I think they went a little too far on that point.' Or 'Where in the world did *that* come from?' Then I would go to the Scripture and read the account, and invariably I would say, 'Wow! That really *is* implied in the text. I never saw that!' "

Little did she realize that when the *Your Story Hour* ministry was starting out, one of their first needs was for a scriptwriter. They contacted Virgil Iles, who was a student at Emmanuel Missionary College and had done some scriptwriting. Initially, he declined, but after considerable persuasion, he agreed to do a sample. He later said, "When I started to write, the words just seemed to flow from my pen, and I knew there was a Power guiding my hand that I had never before experienced in writing scripts."

Susy remembers one of her sons bringing a friend home from college. "I heard this friend, who had little exposure to spiritual things, decrying the moral state of young people. Then he asked our son how we had taught morality. Phil and I did a lot in our family besides *Your Story Hour*—he taught the kids almost daily devotions, we used a Christian curriculum in our homeschool, we were actively involved in our church, we had a child evangelism club in our home that the children helped lead, we played Christian radio much of the time, and through traveling with our own ministry we exposed the children to many of the leading preachers and Christian teachers of the time. But Matt responded by telling his friend about *Your Story Hour* and used as an example the story 'To Kill a Devil,' in which a couple returned kindness repeatedly to a neighbor who was bitter and hateful and had even killed their dog. This young man was fascinated."

Some people are under the mistaken impression that *Your Story Hour* is only for children, but Susy disproved that assumption by encouraging a friend over several years to buy some sets of *Your Story Hour* for his grandchildren. "Roger was president of Christian Business Men's Connection at the time. He finally bought some of the Old Testament series that included Esther and Daniel and said he thought he had better listen to them first to be sure they were OK. He later told me that they were so well-done and fascinating that he had to listen to them a second time before he could part with them!"

Today, nearly seventy years since *Your Story Hour* first began, millions around the world just like the Downers love listening to the inspiring Bible stories, uplifting miracle stories, fascinating historical stories, and exciting adventure stories presented, now broadcast in English, Spanish, and Russian.

*"Blessed are the merciful,
for they will be shown mercy."*

—Matthew 5:7, NIV

Parenting 2.0

Helping Hands Caregiver Resource Center

Lisa didn't know what to do. Her mother, Allene, was no longer able to live independently due to an unexpected mitral valve prolapse. Anxiety, difficulty breathing from chronic asthma, and the aftermath of a complete nervous breakdown had left Allene feeling overwhelmed and unable to cope. Allene could still do many things for herself, but it was difficult for her to do necessary daily tasks such as cooking meals or doing laundry. Her doctors felt it would be best if she lived with someone who could help, so Allene moved in with Lisa.

For a while, it was a wonderful arrangement for both. Allene attended a local adult day care program during the day while Lisa worked. Allene was safe and well cared for. She was able to socialize with friends and enjoyed an exercise regime to maintain her mobility. Professional medical staff managed her health needs.

All seemed to be going well until the program lost funding and suddenly closed. Lisa didn't know what to do, and along with many other families caring for a loved one, fear of having to admit her mom to a long-term care facility filled her with apprehension. Lisa's love for her mom and the reality that they couldn't afford in-home care or the cost of a facility overwhelmed her with worry. She was desperate to find a solution. How could she afford to pay someone to stay with her mom on her limited income? What would her family think if she was forced to put her mom in a nursing home? Would her mom feel abandoned and unwanted? Would her mom even love her anymore? How could she live with herself if she made the wrong decision? These and other questions flooded her mind with panic. It was a very difficult, uncertain time.

That's when Helping Hands Caregiver Resource Center, a ministry of the Penn Valley Seventh-day Adventist Church, stepped in. God impressed the hearts of the pastor and members of the Penn Valley Church to provide what was no longer available: a place of rest and compassion. The plan to serve in this capacity was appealing to the church members and spiritually relevant to their mission of community service and ministry. It supplied the calm needed by families weathering the storm of caring for their aging or disabled loved ones.

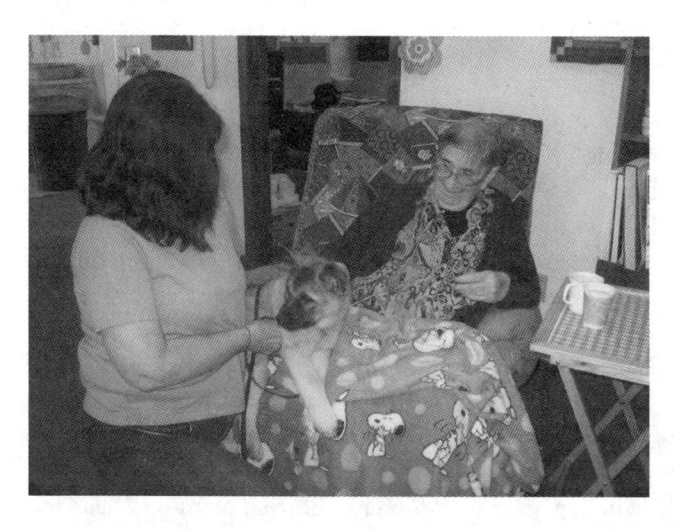

Allene enjoys pet therapy with the puppy. This was taken just a couple of weeks before she passed away (2017).

A respite care ministry is a unique opportunity to connect with families and caregivers who are often unseen in society. Adult day care programs are state-licensed and regulated. Participants in adult day care programs find compassion, friendship, encouragement, improved self-esteem, and independence. In Nevada County, Helping Hands Caregiver Resource Center is a beacon of hope for caregivers of dependent adults. The caregivers get a much-needed respite, and their loved ones enjoy a warm, caring environment. The role of caring for a loved one at home can cause isolation that often goes unnoticed to others outside. As the nation's population ages, and with early onset dementia diseases on the rise, more and more adults are having their needs met by adult family members who live in the home. Often this results in hardship as children of aging parents continue to work full-time jobs to provide for their own needs. The demands of caregiving can lead to withdrawal from normal social activities. The average caregiver often has many roles to fill and, without help and support, can quickly become overwhelmed, depressed, and even physically ill.

It is a prevailing belief that caring for elderly family members is the adult child's responsibility. In North America, institutionalization offers a viable option—but at a high price. For the many who desperately need to find a way to stay at home, the financial and emotional burden multiplies drastically. Families struggle to balance what they can afford to provide and a quality of life that maintains dignity and respect. Through the ministry of respite, these families receive kindness and compassion.

Allene told people that "being at Helping Hands was far better than being at home."

When they asked why, she replied, "Because I don't like being left alone, and here I have so many friends!"

She brought laughter and joy to the other participants as they arrived each morning by singing the 1918 Irving Berlin song "Oh, How I Hate to Get up in the Morning." Occasionally they would purposely groan at her singing, but it was always in the spirit of fun.

Allene also suffered from bipolar disorder. During her lifetime she'd struggled through many ups and downs of depression. Often, she would isolate herself and spend time reading, watching movies, or painting. Being in crowded places around strangers increased her anxiety. She felt safe at Helping Hands, and whenever she was having an episode of depression, she would sit quietly and color pictures. She used colored pencils to draw beautiful abstract landscape scenes or animals she loved. This solo activity helped her cope while still keeping her connected with others. Allene would draw strength from her peers as they recognized her need for quiet healing. She applied her own "medicine" of happiness by gifting her art to friends and program family. Even now, Lisa finds a sense of calmness in seeing her mother's drawings. They remind her of how important beauty is in a dark world where pain is ever present and that a simple, heartfelt gift is more meaningful than all the riches in the world.

Allene was fondly nicknamed "Huggy Bear" because she gave warm hugs to everyone she met, and she could always be found in her recliner waiting for someone to come sit and visit with her. Unable to participate in the physically active games, she would often observe and give her perspective on those playing. A lifelong fan of the comic strip character Snoopy, she would interject, "Snoopy could take better aim than that!" whenever someone missed the target in a game of cornhole. Her funny comments made everyone laugh, and her sweet spirit and wonderful sense of humor made her a favorite with everyone at the program.

When someone asked Allene what the best thing about going to Helping Hands was, she replied, "Just to know my daughter can go to work in peace and not worry about me." During her last few months at the program, she required oxygen to breathe. She was thankful and comforted by her program family, who encouraged, supported, and prayed for her.

Allene was eighty-nine when she passed away quietly and at peace. At her memorial service, family members distributed her many Snoopy collector's items. The room was full of laughter and tears as everyone shared stories from the nine years she attended the program. Lisa fully believed that Helping Hands extended her mom's life by giving her a loving "family" to interact with each week. Allene and Lisa were able to maintain positive, enriching relationships with family and the community by being included in the church's respite ministry.

The Penn Valley Seventh-day Adventist Church believed that when Jesus said, "Come to me, all you who are weary and burdened, and I will give you rest" (Matthew 11:28, NIV), He meant they should put those words into action by lifting the burdens of weary caregivers through rest and peace of mind. They continue to pray earnestly that those who find themselves facing a hopeless situation will soon find a spirit of refreshment the way Lisa and Allene did through Helping Hands.

Settling Old Scores

International Children's Care

The day that changed Hugo Cabrera's life began like any other day, but it altered his course forever. Born to a happy, if poor, family in the Dominican Republic, Hugo and his siblings had all their basic needs provided for by loving parents. His mother stayed home to care for the house and children while his father, a hard-working, responsible man, went off to work, sometimes for long hours. In the evening when he came home, there might be a walk with the kids to the park for some baseball, which Hugo loved. Or if his father was too tired, they had long, quiet talks around the supper table where the family ate the meals his mother prepared.

And then one night, his father didn't come home.

At first, no one suspected anything was amiss. The family ate dinner without him, though Hugo felt the absence of his presence like the gap in his mouth after losing a tooth. He was anxious for his father to return, and the dinner table felt lonely without him.

"Everything is fine," their mother said as she tucked them into their beds. "Go to sleep now. Daddy will come and say good night when he gets home. Even if it's late. I promise."

He woke up early the next morning hoping to see his father before he left for work. But to his dismay, not only was his father not home, but worse, the house was filled with adults, many of them crying. Panic gripped Hugo's heart. Something bad had happened to his father. He knew it without being told.

He learned that a drunken man, one of his father's best friends, had killed him on his way home the night before.

In a heartbeat, the little family's world changed. Grieving and distraught, Hugo's mother was desperate to feed her fatherless children. She began to take work wherever she could find it. She no longer had time to cook nourishing meals for her family, and the pleasant chats around the table and walks to the park vanished overnight.

Survival became their paramount goal. Even the children had to help. Hugo and his older brother did odd jobs for anyone who would pay them, and they trekked up into the hills in search of firewood to sell in town so that they could buy food. But it was not enough.

Desperate, Hugo's mother realized that if she did not get help, her little family would starve. It was with severe hunger pains that they made their way to the International Children's Care Las Palmas Children's Village.

International Children's Care is a charitable organization whose goal is helping the world's homeless children, particularly those in developing countries. Their unique philosophy of caring for children in a family setting rather than an institutional one sets them apart and contributes to the success of their mission to take broken lives and make them whole again.

Hugo and his siblings were welcomed by smiling, kind caregivers, and for the first time since his father died, Hugo began to feel safe. They were placed in one of the country home cottages with houseparents to care for them. While Hugo rejoiced that he and his siblings were safe, he mourned the loss of his father and the family life they had shared, which had been ripped away by a selfish, drunken man. Bitterness and hatred took root in his heart, and he decided to make that man pay for what he'd done to Hugo's family. He determined to take the man's life—an eye for an eye.

Hugo nursed these vengeful fantasies as he grew up, imagining all the ways he could kill his father's murderer. At the same time, he was attending church with his new family. He sang Bible songs and listened to Bible stories with the other children, but in his heart, he didn't believe in God or see any value in prayer. When the pastor made altar calls, some of his friends answered and eventually began preparing for baptism. Hugo was willing to respect their decisions, but he knew that if he accepted Jesus in his heart, he would have to turn his back on his plans for revenge. He couldn't let his father down; he had to avenge his death.

One day, as the family prepared for church, Hugo was struck by the changes that had come to him and his siblings since the day they had arrived at the children's village dirty, hungry, sick, and hopeless. If only his father could see them now, he thought wistfully. For a moment his heart softened as he remembered the lessons his International Children's Care housefather had tried to teach him and how patient he had been with Hugo throughout the years.

There was a new speaker at church that day; an energetic young preacher had come to lead a week of prayer for the kids. He didn't use any big words or fancy talk. His message was simply about the immeasurable love of God and the forgiving blood of Jesus.

As the congregation began to sing that day, Hugo felt a shift in the hardness of his heart. A crack developed and widened as the congregation began to sing "Whiter Than Snow." He had a sudden conviction that the words had been written just for him. He began to sing with feeling, the song becoming a prayer. Trembling, he made his way to the front at the altar call and dropped to his knees. He was baptized the following Sabbath, but before his baptism, he made a pact with the Lord.

"Lord," he said, "I have lived with hate all my life. I have fostered murderous plans in my heart. Please help me forgive the man who killed my father. I will serve you in whatever capacity I can if you help me overcome."

Hugo's life changed dramatically. He graduated from high school, went to college, fell in love, got married, and moved to New York City, far away from his past. Or so he thought. One day he informed his wife that he needed to go back to the Dominican Republic, and he needed to go alone.

Memory after memory assaulted him as he made his way to the old town and neighborhood he had lived in when he was a child. Standing at the door of his father's killer, he knocked deliberately. A weak old man answered and stared at him with rheumy, sunken eyes. Hugo realized that the man had no idea who he was.

"I am Hugo Cabrera," Hugo explained. "You don't remember me, but you killed my father when I was a very little boy. As a child, I made a pledge that one day I would find you and avenge my father's blood." He paused for a second to swallow. His throat felt tight and dry. "Even though what you did to my father hurt us deeply, God never abandoned us." He noticed the old man shaking uncontrollably like someone experiencing great torment. "God brought us to a home for orphaned and abandoned children run by kind Christian people who loved us and taught us love and kindness. They introduced us to Jesus, in whom I found salvation. For many years I fantasized about the day that I would come and kill you the same way you killed my father, but when I gave my life to Jesus, He took away all my hate. Today I am here to tell you that I have forgiven you. Don't torture yourself any longer with guilt, because I am forgiving you for what you did. Furthermore, I would like to invite you to accept Jesus as your Savior and confess all your sins to Him and give Him all your past so that you may experience the peace that I experience today."

The man looked at Hugo, not knowing what to say or do.

"I had to do it," Hugo told his wife when he returned. "For my own sake and for the sake of the old man, I had to do it. I can only imagine the daily torment in his heart as he thought about what he had done. And I'll tell you something: there is nothing more beautiful than the power of forgiveness."

The Witch of Barillal

Water for Life International

Barillal is a little village in Guatemala almost at the end of the road near the border of Belize. Several homes are close to the road, but the majority of homes (or what pass for homes in that area) are not on the road, but are down the many paths that lead off the road into the dense jungle. The board of Water for Life International, a Washington-based nonprofit organization dedicated to providing clean, potable water to remote villages in northeast Guatemala, had purchased land and built a small church in Barillal several years prior. Berny Leonardo was there checking on a well that had been drilled in the yard of the Adventist church.

As he tested the hand pump, a woman came toward him, greeted him, and asked whether he could come to help a little girl. Berny asked what was wrong.

"Snakebite," the woman replied bleakly.

Berny did not have any medical supplies, but he immediately agreed to go and started walking with the woman down one of the paths into the jungle in the steamy heat. As they walked, Berny learned that the woman was the little girl's aunt and that the little girl had been bitten the day before. She had no parents, and she stayed with her grandmother. He asked about the snake, but no one had seen it.

After walking about ten minutes, maybe a few hundred meters (a few hundred yards), they came to a small clearing in the jungle. Here several homes had been put together from various wood scraps: a piece of plywood and some boards for walls and a few pieces of rusted metal with some thatch for a roof. The floors were dirt, and the furnishings were a few plastic crates and an old folding chair. In the corner was a firepit. It was a typical home for jungle folks. Chickens wandered in and around the house.

The little girl lay on the floor in the corner. Berny checked her over and knew that if she didn't get help, she'd most likely die. He put some water on a dirty cloth and wiped her fevered forehead and checked her pulse. It was weak and fast.

After a few moments, he stood up. Several people were outside the door of the

The Witch of Barillal

shack looking in, and the little girl's grandmother sat in a corner of the shack. He told the grandmother and the aunt that the little girl had to be taken to the doctor, but the aunt just shrugged and said, "No money." Berny understood. In Guatemala, if you did not have money and lived in the jungle, there was no help.

Berny thought for a minute. If he tried to help this little girl and she died, he would be blamed, but if he did nothing, she would surely die. He knew he must try.

"If you'll let me, I'll take her to the hospital in Poptún," he told the aunt and grandmother.

The grandmother waved her hand and said, "Go, but she will die."

Berny scooped up the sick little girl in his arms and began walking back to his truck in the churchyard with the girl's aunt. When they reached the truck, Berny placed the little girl across the back seat, and the aunt got in with her and put the child's head on her lap. Berny started the hour-and-a-half drive to town. As he drove as fast as he could on the rutted road, he and the aunt talked. He learned the little girl's grandmother was the village witch and that she had done all she knew to make the girl well. When the child had not responded, she had predicted the girl would surely die and declared that the spirits were punishing someone.

Berny sent up quiet prayers as he drove. After they had been traveling about an hour and were in a place familiar to Berny, he came to the house of a man who was skilled in the use of natural medicine. He stopped briefly to see if the man had anything to help the child. When the man came out to the truck, Berny told him what he knew, and the man looked at the girl, felt her skin, and saw the two small marks. He quietly told Berny that the little girl was probably going to die and mentioned that he thought the snake was a *barba amarilla*, or fer-de-lance, an extremely venomous pit viper whose bite was often deadly. Berny knew that very little could be done for someone who had been bitten by one of those snakes, but he would do whatever he could. The man made a poultice out of some leaves and put it on the bite. Then he told Berny to hurry to the hospital.

Thirty minutes later they made it to Poptún, and Berny pulled up to the government hospital. The people at the hospital knew Berny from his work with Water for Life International, and they immediately took the little girl in to be examined by the doctor while Berny talked with the business office about the expenses. He told them to do whatever was necessary and that Water for Life International would pay for her care. He told the aunt to stay with her, gave her a few *quetzales* (Guatemalan money), and said he would be back the next day to check on her.

The following day he stopped by. The aunt was there, and the child, though resting more comfortably, was still very sick. She was still in danger but was holding on. The only thing they could do was to continue to support her and hope she would survive.

Maybe there was nothing *they* could do, but Berny knew what *he* could do. He went to the local church pastor and asked him to gather the church people and

Tim Rasmussen, president of Water for Life International, poses with the little girl from Barillal, Guatemala.

have a special session of prayer for the little girl. The pastor agreed and spread the word to all the church people in the area to pray for the little girl.

For three days, every time Berny stopped by, the little girl was doing better. Eventually, it became obvious that she would survive. After five days, the hospital said she could go home. Berny paid the hospital bill and helped them on their way.

Several months later, Berny needed to go to Barillal again to help with some Sabbath School classes and to bring some plastic chairs for the church. As he drove out on Sabbath morning, he wondered whether he would see the little girl he had helped. When he got to the village, he unloaded the chairs and joined in the singing.

As he looked around, he saw the little girl happily taking part in the children's songs and listening intently at story time. The girl's aunt was also in the congregation. After the service, he spoke to the child. She was shy with him, but when she realized he was the one who had taken her to the doctor, she hugged his leg for a moment before running off.

The aunt motioned to Berny to come and meet the grandmother. Berny thought she meant for him to walk out into the brush again and he hesitated, but no, the grandmother was just outside; she had come to church that day. She greeted Berny warmly and thanked him for saving her grandchild; they talked for a few minutes about that ordeal months before.

Later, Berny talked to the Bible worker in the area and learned that the grandmother had been coming to church and taking Bible studies. He kept in touch with the village and the Bible worker and, about a year later, was excited to learn that the aunt and grandmother were going to be baptized. The witch of Barillal became a Seventh-day Adventist!

Doctor, Come Quickly!

Scheer Memorial Adventist Hospital

"Doctor, come quickly! The patient admitted with alcohol withdrawal is seizing."

Dr. Dale Molé, chief executive officer at Scheer Memorial Adventist Hospital in Nepal, had just finished eating Sabbath lunch with Dr. Jonathon Thorp, who was an internal medicine doctor at Scheer, Dr. Thorp's family, and a guest. They had been discussing some of the tragic cases of suicide they had cared for at Scheer Memorial Hospital. Suicide, especially among young people, was reaching a crisis level in the Kavre District, where the hospital is located. Among the rural populations, poverty and despair result in a suicide rate nearly four times what it was ten years ago. Scheer Memorial Hospital provides wholistic care to residents in Benepa, Nepal, and is the only hospital in the district willing to treat those desperate individuals.

Drs. Molé and Thorp rushed straight to the intensive care unit. They found the staff struggling to resuscitate a twenty-five-year-old man, Raju,* who had been admitted a few hours earlier with a diagnosis of alcohol withdrawal. He was now seizing, and copious amounts of foam coming from his lungs streamed out of his mouth. The symptoms didn't fit the clinical picture of a simple alcohol withdrawal seizure. As the doctors tried to figure out what was happening, they stabilized his airway, administered drugs for the seizure, and inserted an endotracheal tube in his airway. Dr. Thorp soon realized what they were seeing wasn't an alcohol withdrawal seizure as they had been told. Instead, the symptoms were more like the seizures and increased secretions seen with poisoning from organophosphate, a common pesticide used in farming in Nepal.

That type of poisoning produced the same symptoms as a military nerve agent or nerve gas. It was extremely difficult to save someone's life if they had ingested this poison; a rapid diagnosis was essential for a successful outcome. The patient's lack of candor confounded the diagnosis, making it much more challenging.

---

* Name changed.

Scheer Memorial Hospital

Raju had tried to take his own life by drinking insecticide, and he very nearly succeeded.

Over the next ninety minutes, Raju received massive doses of atropine, the antidote for that poison. For perspective, most of the poisoning cases the hospital treats require fifty to seventy-five milliliters of atropine, but Raju required almost five times that much.

He remained in the ICU (intensive care unit) for the next two weeks, requiring a lot of nursing care. Raju survived by God's grace and the treatment provided by the dedicated staff at the mission hospital. Raju still needed healing—healing of his soul. That was something only God could provide.

In another part of the hospital, little Rijan was dying. The eleven-year-old Nepali boy had been sick with typhoid fever for days. Travel was difficult in Nepal, so by the time he arrived at the emergency room, the infection had already overwhelmed his body. Pale skin, a bounding pulse, fever, and low blood pressure told the doctors he was in septic shock, a life-threatening condition.

Without a moment to waste, doctors rushed him to the operating room. They opened his distended abdomen and found it filled with pus. The untreated typhoid infection had caused a small hole in his intestines, allowing the intestinal contents to spill out into his abdomen, spreading the infection. After much searching, the surgeon was able to find the hole and carefully suture it closed. Then they washed his abdominal cavity with massive quantities of a sterile solution in the hope of flushing away any remaining infection. After surgery, his frail body was transferred to the ICU in critical condition.

Rijan was fighting for his life, and the odds of survival were not in his favor.

Later, Dr. Molé stopped by the ICU to see how he was doing. While talking with the nursing staff, Dr. Molé noticed the monitor displaying the level of oxygen in Rijan's blood, which was slowly drifting lower and lower. Rijan was developing acute respiratory distress syndrome, a common complication of septic shock. His little lungs were filling with fluid and preventing oxygen from getting into his blood. A portable chest X-ray confirmed their worst fears.

Acute respiratory distress syndrome is highly lethal, especially when combined with septic shock. The hospital staff rushed to address these new problems by inserting an endotracheal tube into his airway, providing breathing support with a mechanical ventilator, and giving him pure oxygen in an effort to improve the amount reaching his starving tissues. They were doing everything they could, but despite their best efforts, it was unlikely the little boy would survive the night.

As Rijan struggled for his life, the doctors and nurses, who had exhausted all the treatments available at their hospital, gathered around his bed to pray that his life might be spared. His family was crying outside the ICU in anticipation of what the future held for their precious little boy. Dr. Molé left the ICU with a heavy heart that night. He was almost certain that when he returned in the morning, Rijan's bed would be empty, his life cut short by poverty and ignorance—a future scientist, engineer, doctor, or teacher who would never live to help his country join the community of developed nations.

That night sleep was difficult. It was hard for Dr. Molé to fathom how, in the twenty-first century, with all the advances in science and medicine, an innocent child might die from typhoid fever, a disease all but eradicated from developed nations through the benefits of modern sanitation and a robust health-care system.

As soon as he woke up the next morning, Dr. Molé rushed to the ICU to see how little Rijan was doing. To his surprise, he found the critically ill patient not only alive but requiring less oxygen than just a few hours previously. Throughout the day Dr. Molé continued to check on Rijan's condition. To his utter amazement and joy, the boy's condition continued to improve. Slowly, doctors lowered his oxygen concentration and then removed the ventilator completely.

Remarkably, a few days later he was out of the ICU and smiling from his bed in the pediatric ward. It was truly a miracle! According to medical science, Rijan should have died. But God had different plans for him.

Dr. Molé realized then why he had sold his home in the United States, put all his worldly goods in storage, and moved halfway across the world to one of the world's poorest and least-developed countries to treat Rijan and others like him. God had been preparing him for mission service since he was a little boy about the same age as Rijan. Now here he was, working side by side with God to change the lives of the "least of these" in a hospital dedicated to saving both the body and the soul.

Answering the Call

International Children's Care

"You are caring for abandoned children there at El Oasis, aren't you? Couldn't you find room for Vanessa? She is a sweet little girl and needs and wants a home so much."

Pastor Reyes had answered the urgent phone call and recognized the voice of one of his former secretaries.

"Tell me more about Vanessa's story. We will do everything we can to help," he responded.

For thirty-three years, International Children's Care (ICC) had been taking in abandoned, rejected, and orphaned children. From its humble beginning of meeting a need in Guatemala after a devastating earthquake left many children homeless, ICC had grown and spread to many other areas of need in the world. Pastor Reyes worked with the El Oasis Children's Village in Mexico. As he listened, he heard a familiar story.

Vanessa had never been accepted by her family. Her mother left her father when Vanessa, the youngest of five children, was very small. Neither of her parents wanted her. After they separated, her mother married a divorced man who had a daughter living with him. To please her new husband, she began focusing on his daughter and neglecting Vanessa. The stepfather decided he didn't want Vanessa living with them, so her mother took her to live with her grandmother.

Vanessa's grandmother was old and poor and unable to care for a child, so Vanessa didn't go to school but wandered around the streets all day. The girl had never learned to read. After several years, the grandmother got sick and could no longer have Vanessa living with her, so she sent her back to her mother. Her mother still didn't want her and began to abuse her to such an extent that some neighbors called the police. Vanessa's mother spent six months in jail. The National System for Integral Family Development (in Spanish: Sistema Nacional para el Desarrollo Integral de la Familia; SNDIF or just DIF), a Mexican public institution for social assistance that focuses on strengthening and developing Mexican families, took Vanessa to an orphanage in another part of

Mexico. Again, the little girl suffered abuse. DIF removed her and began looking for a better home for her.

As Pastor Reyes listened, the woman continued, "I have always loved Vanessa and would love to give her a home. I told this to DIF, but the authorities felt that Vanessa needed a home with a full-time mother."

When Pastor Reyes called DIF, they were very happy to approve Vanessa going to live at El Oasis. The mother, grandmother, and uncle brought her. At last Vanessa had found a home where she was welcomed and loved. She proved to be a happy and cooperative little girl.

Just three days after Vanessa arrived at El Oasis, she celebrated her birthday. She looked in awe at the beautiful cake. Then her eyes rested on the brightly wrapped package beside the cake.

Pastor Mauro Reyes

"Is that really for me?" she exclaimed.

One of ICC's founding principles is that their program would not resemble a typical orphanage. Instead of housing many children in one building, they place children in individual homes built on small acreages. National couples serve as parents to groups of ten to twelve children, each unit forming a family. Their long-term results have proven positive, helping children learn basic skills and relate to life in a more normal way.

ICC's basic plans for each children's country village include ten homes for children, an administration building, an elementary school, and a shop or industrial building. In some cases, there is also a centrally located receiving center where the children are first processed and where children who are sick or have special needs are housed temporarily. There is also a farm, which provides work opportunities for older children. It also provides food and lessens the need for outside help. Also, the children learn manual skills, thus preparing each child for independent living.

Of equal importance to the love and care given to the children is the spiritual emphasis in the home. Christian principles guide each home. "Parents" tailor morning and evening worship to the interests of small children. In an atmosphere of Christlike love and compassion, with godly parents as role models, the children learn to be true Christians with the Bible as the foundation of their faith.

Shortly after arriving at El Oasis, Vanessa went timidly to her new housemother. "There is something I would like to talk with you about, Mrs. Rodriguez."

The El Oasis House. International Children's Care provides family-unit style residences for the children in its care.

"Yes, *mi hijita* (my daughter), what is it?" Mrs. Rodriguez led Vanessa over to the couch and sat down with her, holding her hand between her own hands.

"I have never really had a mother that I could call 'Mommy.' Would it be all right with you if I called you 'Mommy'?" She looked up with a tear trickling down her cheek.

"Oh, *mi hijita*, of course you can call me 'Mommy'! That is a great honor for me, and I really want you to understand that you now have a real family with a mommy and daddy. And you can come and talk with me anytime. I love you!"

As they embraced in that special moment, Mrs. Rodriguez knew that once again God had worked a special miracle in the life of a child. She remembered that He is the Father of the fatherless and by divine providence had led in the establishment of ICC to care for His children on earth.

Many children like Vanessa, who have never been accepted or loved or who possibly are hungry and abused, have arrived on the doorstep of a children's home run by ICC where they can feel secure and loved at last. Unfortunately, many children in the world are wandering around or stuck in abusive situations, children who are the victims of the sin and suffering in this world. ICC provides a place where these children will not only find love and security but will also learn about a God who is the Father of the fatherless.

Each answered phone call has the potential to bring another child home.

Delivered From Desperation

Helping Hands Caregiver Resource Center

Larry worked as a housepainter in California with his father-in-law to support his family. He and his wife, whom he had married at eighteen, had three daughters. He had no ambition to continue his education, but raising a family wasn't his idea of a successful life, either. Soon he took up drinking alcohol, abusing it for many years. Because of his alcoholism, his wife divorced him, he lost his job, and he and his daughters became estranged.

Then Larry mysteriously disappeared.

Beginning sometime in 1998, nobody knew where he was or where he might have gone. Seven years passed. The mystery nagged at Larry's daughter Angela. She decided to stop wondering what might have happened to her father and hired a private investigator. The investigator discovered that Larry was living in a care home in Philadelphia, where he had been placed five years earlier after having a stroke caused by his chronic alcoholism. The stroke had left him handicapped with dementia, impaired mobility, and seizures. Angela was relieved to finally know where her father was and that he was still alive.

Larry's ex-wife and her close friend, Joyce, decided to bring him back home to California. In his condition, he could not live alone, so they decided he would live in Joyce's home since she was already taking care of a family member, and her home was right next door to Angela's house. Joyce became Larry's full-time caregiver, but caring for two grown adults with multiple needs was overwhelming. Joyce was busy twenty-four hours a day, without any free time for herself.

Larry was uncommunicative, a symptom of severe depression from his dependent condition and isolation. When he was evaluated, a county social service nurse suggested that if Larry would attend the Helping Hands Caregiver Resource Center's adult day social program, it would give Joyce a much-needed break and Larry some socialization. Helping Hands, a state-licensed adult day care program owned and operated by the Penn Valley Seventh-day Adventist Church, was a ministry that had been created for just that purpose: to give dependent adults a stimulating social environment while providing their caregivers respite with peace of mind.

Baking cupcakes for others at Helping Hands Caregiver Resource Center helped bring Larry out of his depression.

From Larry's very first day at the program, everyone thought he couldn't talk. He would arrive on the paratransit bus, shuffle across the room using his walker for balance, and sit at a table as far away from everyone as possible. Day after day he sat there, watching the activity around him but not joining in. That didn't stop the other participants or staff from approaching him with a greeting. Joyfully they would attempt to interact with him and, in return, receive a silent nod or blank stare.

For many months this pattern repeated. Larry was physically there, but no one was able to get him to engage socially. They believed his stroke had affected his ability to communicate and interact with people. Joyce had told the staff that Larry seldom said anything. But what truly broke everyone's heart was his demeanor of great sadness and despair. His depression seemed to be almost literally eating his soul, and he seemed helpless to pull himself up out of the darkness. Everyone tried to entice him to participate, but Larry couldn't even try.

While everyone else was playing games, laughing, and creating art projects, he sat silently, watching. However, when the weekly musical program came through, he had no choice but to listen. Through the universal language of music, Larry began to show some interest in life again and exhibit a little hope. He started to respond when his peers greeted him. Though most people wouldn't have noticed, it was obvious to those at the program that subtle changes were happening.

At that point, Larry had been attending the program for two years, but the staff had been unable to cajole him into participating in the activities they planned. During a staff meeting one month, a lengthy discussion revolved around ways to engage Larry. The program director suggested starting a weekly activity called the Director's Club. The next week the director came in to the program late morning and announced that the Director's Club would be making cupcakes. Participants were busy with a craft activity, and none of them wanted to be involved, so the director approached Larry, sitting silently at his table looking through the newspaper.

"Larry, can you help me make cupcakes this morning?" the director asked. Larry slowly turned his gaze to her face and made no response. "Larry, I really need your help to get this project done. It's for today's dessert, and everyone will be disappointed if we don't have something to serve. Will you please help me?"

Slowly Larry nodded. Quickly the director gathered the materials needed, fully expecting Larry to disengage and simply watch her make the batter. But he surprised her—and everyone else—when he took hold of the spoon and slowly stirred the ingredients as she added them to the bowl. In between adding wet ingredients to the flour mixture, she would ask for Larry's opinion.

"Does the batter look right? Is it thick enough, or should we add more milk?" Larry would nod or say, "Yes, it's good."

She encouraged him too. "Stirring it by hand is far better than using the mixer. I bet it's going to taste like homemade love when you're done."

Larry's demeanor began to evolve from sad and defeated to what looked suspiciously like satisfaction. When they completed the project, with cupcakes ready to go into the oven, Larry simply said, "Thank you. Can we do this again?"

From that day on, Larry started to change in a positive way. He began to show interest in what was going on. He joined in conversations at his table, and over the next three years, it was obvious the depression was lessening. Eventually, Larry started playing dominoes with a few of the guys. He also contributed to trivia games or crossword puzzles the group worked on together. He seldom smiled, but his eyes twinkled when he enjoyed something or heard a funny story and everyone else laughed. He formed meaningful friendships with the other participants. They became his family, along with Joyce, who had been relieved from the burden of caring for him all the time.

During the latter part of 2017, Larry became ill. He stopped eating and began losing weight. Everyone was concerned, and when Larry was diagnosed with lung cancer, it was devastating for all. He continued to attend the program, but now weakness prevented him from expending any energy. Staff and participants alike prayed for him and for Joyce, who was constantly worried about him. The time came when he could no longer attend. He was very ill and admitted to a skilled nursing facility for constant pain relief and terminal care. He required a tracheotomy just to breathe.

During his last few days, he constantly asked if he could return to the program one last time. When asked why, he replied, "I just can't leave without saying goodbye to my friends." Sadly, Larry was unable to say goodbye to so many who had grown to love him.

Though Larry was a quiet and quirky man, the staff at Helping Hands felt that through his eyes they learned to listen and observe others and appreciate who they were as people and not simply as people with disabilities. Larry had found much more than a home and family when he arrived at Helping Hands. He found hope in living in the present because nobody judged him for his past.

Helping Hands demonstrated that compassionate ministry reveals the character of Christ through how we relate with and care about others. Reaching people's hearts through service, Helping Hands strives to serve "the least of these" in the same way Jesus did.

> *"Blessed are the pure in heart,
> for they will see God."*
>
> —Matthew 5:8, NIV

Buried Alive

Scheer Memorial Adventist Hospital

It was just past noon on a beautiful spring Sabbath, April 25, 2015, in Banepa, Nepal. The largest Adventist congregation in the country had finished song service, offering, opening prayer, and special music in the little church on the Scheer Memorial Adventist Hospital campus. The Sabbath speaker had just approached the pulpit to deliver God's message when the rumbling tremor began.

A hush fell over the congregation as they stared in silent bewilderment at one another, trying to comprehend what was happening as the once solid ground beneath their feet continued to shake stronger and stronger. Should they stay put or run outside? Overwhelmed by fear of being crushed, they quickly ran outside, only to be greeted by the sound of collapsing buildings, screams, and cries for help. Clouds of dust now filled the air. The most powerful earthquake in more than eighty years—7.8 magnitude—had just ended thousands of lives and displaced 2.8 million people in a matter of seconds. The final tally was 8,617 killed and 16,808 injured. In all, the number of people affected was 5.6 million. More than 473,000 houses were destroyed.*

Patients who could walk started streaming out of the hospital wards because no one wanted to stay inside. The injured arrived on foot and by motorcycle, car, and truck, and a few, by ambulance. Medical staff resuscitated patients outside on the hospital grounds. Nine were dead on arrival with massive head injuries. The hospital evacuated all patients from the hospital and set up temporary inpatient wards outside.

But even amidst all the death and destruction, new life entered the world. A pregnant woman required an emergency cesarean section when the earthquake struck. Two missionaries, one an anesthesiologist and the other an obstetrics and gynecology doctor, rolled the patient and anesthesia equipment outside into the hospital courtyard. After a quick prayer, they operated beneath the open sky in view of the doctors, surgical staff, and a few birds sitting in nearby trees. Soon the

---

* Mark Leon Goldberg, "Nepal Earthquake Facts and Figures," UN Dispatch, May 19, 2015, https://www.undispatch.com/nepal-earthquake-facts-and-figures/.

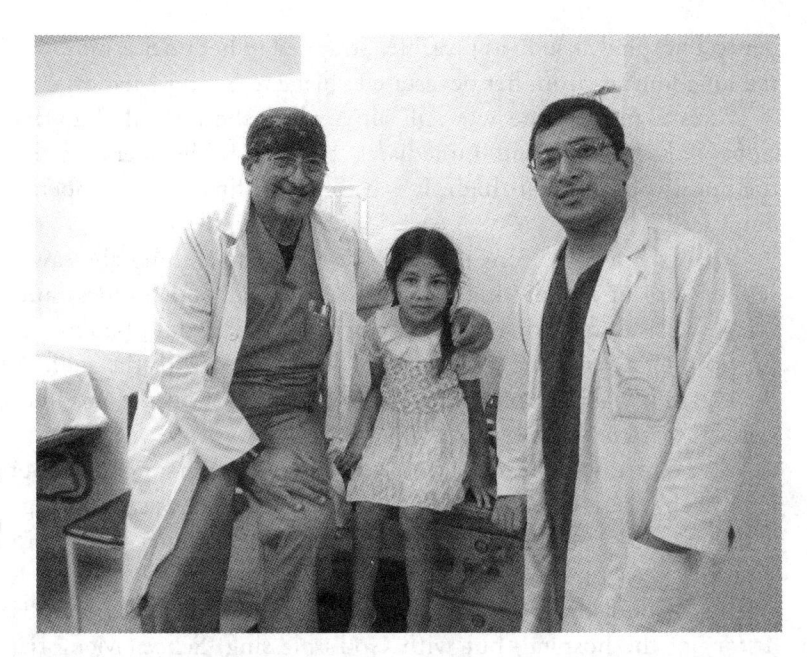

Nine-year-old Soniya survived a 2015 earthquake in Nepal thanks in part to receiving critical care at Scheer Memorial Hospital.

sound of new human life filled the courtyard. What amazed the missionary doctors was the parting of the overcast sky just before the surgery started. Sunlight streamed down from the heavens and illuminated the patient and the surgical field. Almost as soon as the operation ended, the clouds rolled back in. Both mother and baby did well.

When another major earthquake struck Nepal on May 12, fewer died, but the patients still insisted on staying in tents on the hospital grounds. Gradually, staff members convinced them it was safe to return to the inpatient wards.

Over the following weeks, more than one thousand earthquake victims received care at Scheer Memorial Hospital. One of them was nine-year-old Soniya, who had been playing in the yard with her family and decided to go into the house to wash her hands. When the quake struck, her world came crashing down, literally, when the house collapsed on top of her. Looking in horror at the rubble, her family immediately assumed she had been killed along with the thousands of others who died that day.

But little Soniya was not dead. Although badly injured and trapped beneath piles of rubble, she survived. When she heard her grandfather talking about her and crying, she gathered the strength to call out, "I am not dead. Stop talking and get me out of here!" The family was overjoyed but also realized that unless they were able to dig her out soon, she would perish. Frantically, they began digging toward the weak voice of their precious, entombed child, stopping periodically to listen and verify that she was still alive.

After struggling nearly two hours, they finally freed Soniya. Barely alive, she had a serious thigh injury and had lost a lot of blood. Their only hope was to get her to a hospital as soon as possible. Strapped to her uncle's motorcycle, she made the long journey from her devastated village to Scheer Memorial.

It was a miracle she was still alive when she arrived. The doctors quickly stopped the bleeding and immediately took her to the operating theater to repair the huge wound in her thigh. It was to be the first of many operations for little Soniya.

When she awoke from the anesthesia, the first thing she saw was the tear-stained face of her mother. They were tears of both sadness and joy, for she knew that the road to recovery for her daughter would be long. Soniya was in the hospital a very long time and quickly bonded with the staff. When she saw the children walking to the Esa Memorial School on the hospital campus, she yearned to go to school too.

Word of her desire reached the Christian staff, who quickly "adopted" the little family. They purchased a uniform, and soon Soniya was attending school along with her younger brother. The hospital hired her mother to work in the hospital canteen.

The earthquakes that rocked Nepal in 2015 were the worst disasters in the history of the hospital, but with God's blessing, Scheer Memorial had mostly cosmetic damage. A few areas required seismic retrofitting, and one of the badly damaged auxiliary waste management buildings had to be torn down. However, that damage was minor in comparison to many areas of the country, which had been reduced to rubble. Most important in the eyes of the Christian staff was that they were able to demonstrate God's love to the people of Nepal in their time of great need.

Hunt for Success

Mamawi Atosketan Native School

One of the most important young adult milestones for a First Nations (indigenous people groups in Canada) boy is to kill his first deer. But Ethan was eighteen years old, and he had never shot a deer. Ethan didn't have a father who could take him on hunting trips in the Rocky Mountains, the traditional hunting grounds for the Cree people in Alberta, Canada. Ethan lived with his aunt and uncle on a Cree reserve that was about a two-hour drive from the Rocky Mountains. So, Ethan asked his eleventh-grade teacher at Mamawi Atosketan Native School (MANS), Michael Willing, to take him hunting.

Michael knew that the First Nations peoples had a long tradition of sustenance hunting for survival. He also knew that many students didn't have an opportunity to go hunting.

"I'll take you if you get permission from your family," he agreed.

With the consent of Ethan's uncle, the teenager and his teacher went on several short trips to hunt for grouse, ducks, and geese. Ethan, however, wanted a deer.

On a snowy November day, the pair set out on an all-day hunting trip to the Rocky Mountains. They loaded supplies onto the pickup truck and were on the road before sunrise. The day passed without success; they were unable to find a single deer.

Shortly before sunset, Ethan spotted a deer in the forest, and the two hunters stalked the animal for more than a mile through snow and mud. Finally, they managed to sneak up within fifty yards of him. Ethan aimed his rifle and—*bang!*—felled the deer with a single shot.

A minute of silence filled the air. Ethan, shocked, couldn't believe that he had made his first kill. In his culture, for a youth to make his first kill was a monumental step toward becoming an adult.

Moments later, Ethan was standing over the deer and performing a traditional Cree ritual of thanking the Creator.

"Thank you, Creator, for providing for my family," he said. After the prayer, Ethan broke a cigarette and sprinkled the tobacco over the animal—another Cree ritual.

Then the hunters' thoughts turned toward taking the deer back home. It was getting dark, and they were far from the pickup truck. The deer weighed about one hundred and fifty pounds.

Michael knew that the whole point of hunting was to feed friends and family. It was a community thing. The first deer was a gift for the elders or the hunter's family.

"I want to give this deer to my family," Ethan said. Michael agreed, and together they worked to move the animal. For an hour and a half, they tried to pull the deer through snow and mud. Finally, Michael returned to the pickup to see if he could drive closer to the deer. He got stuck in the mud just as he reached Ethan and the deer.

"We're in the middle of nowhere at night," he said. "This is not good."

For three hours, the two hunters struggled to pull the vehicle out of the mud. There was no cell phone reception, so they couldn't call for help. However, because they had packed emergency supplies, they weren't worried. Michael lit a roaring fire, and Ethan helped prepare a supper of venison and granola bars. Then the two men fell asleep.

They knew the safest thing to do was stay in one spot at night and not get lost by wandering around in the dark. At dawn, they walked forty-five minutes until they found cell phone reception and could alert their families that they were fine. They managed to get out of the mud and take the deer home.

When they were back in civilization, Michael asked Ethan how he had felt about being stuck in the Rocky Mountains at night.

"I was scared," Ethan replied. "But I trust you as a teacher and a guide, and I knew that you would take care of me. Besides, even with all that happened, it was one of the best stories that has ever happened to me, and I will be able to tell it for the rest of my life!"

Ethan had been a high school dropout, barred from the schools on his home reserve. He was sent to live with his aunt in Maskwacis as a last resort, and MANS was his last-chance school. It had been established in 2003 to serve the four bands of the Maskwacis Cree Nation. The violence-free learning community integrates proven practices of physical, mental, spiritual, and social well-being into each day in a distinctly Cree environment.

Community service and leadership development are high priorities. Starting in second grade, students bake and deliver cookies to the off-reserve community. Some students take an annual trip to Port Hardy, British Columbia, to connect with another, non-Cree, First Nations community. The trip exposes them to the outside world (for many, their first trip off the reserve) and gives them experience in leadership, performance, and community service. For example, the group donated two hundred blankets for those who needed them locally (see "Hope's Mission", page 126) and on the reserve near Port Hardy—a life-and-death mission for families who may not have heat in their homes. An option for a sign-language performance group starting in grade six provides positive group experience and opportunities for leadership and travel as well. The group has performed for Adventist church leaders at North American Division meetings.

MANS also offers a nutrition program, a fundamental part of ensuring that each student can focus and has the food necessary to learn and retain information. Any student who asks gets breakfast and lunch without question. Kindergartners have an afternoon snack. Approximately 70 percent of the student body participates in the program.

In addition to providing Alberta curriculum classes, including vocational and industrial arts classes, MANS incorporates programs and services that promote personal and academic success. Culturally relevant classes that teach the Cree language, aboriginal cultures, and outdoor education are intentionally included in the curriculum. An after-school program offers skill- and confidence-building activities such as archery, winter camping, fishing, and sports. Students can earn an Alberta firearms license and a provisional hunter education certificate. These after-school activities are important in minimizing exposure to gangs during a critical time of the day.

Ethan embraced the after-school program, earning an Alberta hunter education certificate and firearms license, and his attitude in the classroom grew positive as well. He began to view graduating from high school as essential to his plans. He loved to cook and planned to become a chef or, perhaps, if he enjoyed industrial arts, a carpenter or electrician. He now realizes that he needs to graduate to get into those programs.

Before he attended MANS, Ethan didn't think that school was all that important. In fact, he had spent very little time in the classroom at the schools he had attended on a reserve west of Maskwacis before he went to live with his aunt. But MANS, he found, was different. His teachers taught and modeled character and leadership skills and had proved they were willing to help him pursue his goals, both cultural and educational. The excellent academic program respected his cultural and academic needs in a safe, caring environment. His time at MANS gave him the tools he would need not only in hunting game but in his hunt for success in life as well.

Ethan was tragically killed during his senior year at MANS. In his two years at MANS, Ethan had changed from an outsider who despised authority to a serious student, a fun-loving friend to all, and a role model for the younger children. Students voted to name a room in their high school for Ethan to honor and remember him and the outstanding young man he became at MANS. Among Ethan's possessions was a handwritten copy of this Bible verse: "I can do all things through Christ who strengthens me" (Philippians 4:13, NKJV).

Truck Exchange

Water for Life International

The 1946 GMC military six-by-six truck under the drilling rig was tired. It had served Water for Life International in Guatemala well from its first days. God had performed a miracle getting it out of the customs yard when it was imported and another miracle the following year when the magneto (generator) failed. Water for Life workers were able to locate the rare replacement part in the United States within an hour of the call from the jungle.

Only the front axle was pulling when the truck was moved from the village of Lourdes. The brakes required a full can of fluid every time the truck moved, and each gear change brought ominous sounds from the transmission as if this shift might be the last. The smoke from the tailpipe was more like the smokescreen of a navy ship as the engine roared its displeasure at being started one more time. The 1950 Bucyrus Erie 22W drilling rig itself was still doing fine seven years after its donation and refurbishment from the kind folks at R. Stadeli and Sons Well and Pump of Silverton, Oregon, but it was time to find a new truck to carry it.

Bucky Mowery, a faithful volunteer, found a newer truck in Ohio and refurbished it. The truck traveled by low trailer from Ohio to Florida, where it then shipped as open cargo on a container ship to Guatemala. From the port, someone drove it to the Water for Life International shop near Poptún. There it waited to shoulder the eight-thousand-pound drill—if volunteers could find a way to move the rig from one truck to the other.

Dave Rutledge cut the old drilling rig cross members free from the chassis of the old truck. The drill was ready to lift—as ready as four tons could be. The next morning, a Tuesday, the process of moving the drilling rig to the new chassis started in earnest at seven-thirty. The team began with prayers for safety and the successful transfer of the valuable tool.

The crew had four jacks—but of three different sizes. Two were the same size, but the other two were different from the first two and from each other. These jacks were usually used for moving houses. They had enough lifting capacity, but each went up a little faster or slower depending on the thread of the screws into the jacks. Hardwood cribbing was stacked and ready for the lift.

Truck Exchange

Since the new truck was taller than the old truck and its tires were larger, the men determined that the rig needed to be lifted fourteen inches to clear the new truck's bed. They calculated that would give about two inches of clearance.

The lifting process progressed slowly. Every two inches, the stack of cribbing had to be increased and the jacks screwed back down to start again. They checked constantly to make sure the rig stayed level while it was being lifted. There was no margin for error. If something happened and the rig fell, aside from the danger of death to anyone nearby, there would be no way to pick it up again. It would have to be cut up just to be removed from the shop. They did not want the old machine to die needlessly.

Finally, about eight hours later, the rig was fourteen inches higher than it had been when the men started. The rig was suspended in the air about three feet, supported only on stacks of cribbing and four bottle jacks. They pulled out the old truck and gingerly inched in the new chassis. The clearance was just a little over one inch. Any nudge of the suspended rig could be disastrous.

Once the new truck was underneath the rig, the crew used a forklift to adjust the truck chassis about three-quarters of an inch, centering it under the rig left to right. After it was centered, they gently lowered the drilling rig into position on the new chassis. Everyone sighed with relief when the new truck was safely under the rig and it was lowered to meet its new transport.

Dave Rutledge and Monte Johnson spent the next day welding the drilling rig to the truck frame. They worked their way around the rig, Monte grinding to bare clean metal and Dave welding with a steady hand. The men worked steadily and carefully, consulting with each other at every decision during the dangerous job.

Many different people came together for the common goal of providing access to clean water for those who have none. They came from various parts of the country. They possessed diverse skills and qualities. They were of different faiths or none. Though they each had their own reasons for being there, they worked together toward that goal.

The tools are old, the tasks are difficult, the workers are few, but one way or another, Water for Life International overcomes. The Spokane, Washington-based, nonprofit charity is dedicated to providing clean, safe water to remote villages in the Petén region of Guatemala. Because the villages do not have grid power, they drill water wells and equip them with hand pumps. God wants to bring clean water and the gospel of His saving grace—the Living Water—to people who are without either, and Water for Life International is grateful to be His helper.

The Best Gift

Zoz Amba Foundation

Adugnaw Worku was born in rural Ethiopia, destined to live and die in a small, inconsequential village. He inherited subsistence farming as a livelihood, and it was a foregone conclusion that he would be a subsistence farmer like his father, grandfathers, and great-grandfathers. In Adu's village, unpredictable weather patterns and deadly infectious diseases wreaked havoc in everyone's lives.

Life expectancy was very short, and 50 percent of children born in those days died before their fifth birthday. Adu's parents lost eight children, and he almost became the ninth when, at age two, he became so ill that he was pronounced dead.

However, his grandma Belaynesh refused to give up his lifeless body. "His body is still warm, and his skin is still soft," the old lady insisted. "I have seen and touched dead bodies before, and they are cold and hard."

Eventually, someone noticed a faint ribcage movement, and Adu eventually came back to life. As a result, he grew up with an often-repeated family story that God had saved his life for a reason. He was also told that God must have a special plan or work for him.

At seven years old, he became a shepherd, a rite of passage for boys in rural Ethiopia. At twelve, he became a farmer. His father continued to train him in farming techniques; when he was fifteen, his father would give him rigorous tests to see whether he was ready to go out on his own. However, his farming career came to an abrupt end when disaster struck and changed everything.

One dark, moonless night, Adu was walking with friends through bushy country in single file. Asmare Tebeje was walking in front of him and pulled a thorny branch out of the path and then let it snap back without warning Adu. The branch struck the center of Adu's left eye, destroying the lens, scratching the cornea, and causing a traumatic cataract to develop. There were no health-care centers nearby, so Adu had to endure the excruciating pain for three long weeks. In the end, he was completely blind in his left eye.

Adu's uncle Molla came up with a radical idea.

"The white missionary doctors at the Seventh-day Adventist Hospital in Debre Tabor can fix any problem and cure any disease," he said. "We should send him there."

Adu's family agreed and arranged for him to travel with a group of merchants the long fifty miles to Debre Tabor. Adu expected a miracle, but the doctor who saw him was not an eye specialist and was unable to help. Adu left the hospital dejected and depressed.

As he walked to the gate to leave the beautiful campus, he saw a large group of boys and girls running around, a welcome distraction under the circumstances. They were elementary school students there, and they were in recess. Adu felt an overwhelming desire well up inside him. He wanted to be one of them.

At fifteen years old, he was completely illiterate. He had once asked his father whether he could attend a local priest school but was told never to mention the idea again. Still, he could not shake the strong desire to obtain an education. He prayed and asked God to perform miracles and make it possible for him to attend school.

He had little money, only the clothes on his back and about eighty cents in his pocket. But he was determined. He sent the merchants back with a message for his parents that his eye treatment was going to take a long time. Then he set about trying to exchange labor for room and board. He persevered through discouragement as doors remained closed until at last, at an Adventist school in Gubda, everything fell into place and, at the unlikely age of fifteen, he became a proud and happy first-grader.

Adu managed to barter his way through elementary school until he reached eighth grade, when he met an American missionary family who took him in as a family member and not only educated him through graduate school but also helped his three younger siblings from first grade through college.

After twenty-nine years away from home, he returned to his old village in 2000 for a visit. Although he received a warm welcome, he found himself a stranger in a very familiar place. He was sad to observe firsthand that the weathering of the years, infectious diseases, illiteracy, superstition, and abject poverty had taken a heavy toll on the lives of his people. Was it possible to break this chokehold?

After two months of extensive and intense conversations with his fellow villagers, he returned to the United States with a burden in his heart, determined to do something for his people. He could not have ignored their plight even if he tried. He wanted to build a school in his village and break the vicious cycle of illiteracy, superstition, and poverty. He was a firm believer in education, having experienced its transforming power. He was convinced it would transform their lives and change their lot as well.

From 2000 to 2007, he worked on the idea of building a school in his village, and then in 2008, the Lord opened wide unexpected financial doors. Adu chose well-qualified and well-motivated agents in Ethiopia, and together they designed and demonstrated compelling proposals to potential donors.

They named their foundation Zoz Amba after the steep-sided, flat-topped mountain near Adu's home village in northwest Ethiopia because it seemed like a metaphor of life in rural Ethiopia. They chose the acronym OATS, which stands for ownership, accountability, transparency, and sustainability, for their guiding principles and talking points. Together with their generous partners, they built a school in Adu's village, complete with classrooms, a library, a water well, administrative offices, faculty and staff housing, an assembly hall, science labs, and even a computer lab with thirty computers, all in the middle of nowhere. They installed solar panels to generate electricity for the campus, mesmerizing the rural community, which had never seen such "magic" before. The school became a beacon of hope and enlightenment. Today, five hundred boys and girls attend that rural school, a wonderful success story by any measure.

They realized that a vocational school would be a valuable addition or alternative to the regular school. Rural boys and girls learn to work hard very early in life. Ethiopia had been hard at work building infrastructure throughout the nation, and vocationally trained students were in great demand. Zoz Amba collaborated with the community and the local government to build a vocational school twelve miles from Adu's village.

Today, 1,500 students attend that vocational school. It offers a wide variety of subjects, including auto mechanics, garment and textile, electronics, plumbing, construction, drafting and surveying, road construction, and water well drilling and maintenance. The schools have become game-changers in rural communities that have not known such gifts before. Thousands of young people will be educated year after year, and they will be agents of change in an ancient and largely traditional country like Ethiopia.

In addition to its other work, Zoz Amba distributed hundreds of Bibles and Ellen G. White books and gave away radios with high capacity flash drives loaded with prerecorded Adventist Bible lessons and messages. The radios also received Adventist World Radio broadcasts in the local language.

Soon miracle after miracle began to happen. People who had persecuted Adventists now flocked to the church, wanting to know more about Adventism. New converts joined the church in record numbers. Zoz Amba built an all-purpose building near one of its elementary schools, and that flexible building was a training center by day, group housing by night, and a place of worship during weekends.

To Adu, education was the best gift he ever received. Doing for others what others had done for him was one way, perhaps the only way, to honor and continue their legacy and sacrifice.

Rounds and Around

Adventist Health International

Utterly exhausted, Dr. James Appel had just succumbed to sleep when he was jolted awake by his dog Laila's barking. Koumakoy, the nurse on call, was huddled over him, his weak flashlight beam trained on Dr. Appel's face.

"What is it?" he asked, struggling back to consciousness.

"*Docteur*, there's a new patient, a newborn referred from Abéché," he said in French. "He has no anus, and his abdomen is swollen. He also has malaria."

"I'll be right there." Dr. Appel sat up groggily, trying to orient himself. Using the flashlight on his phone, he searched the inside of the eco-dome where he lived to find his scrubs before going to the hospital. The house, like the hospital, had been built with California Institute of Earth Architecture (CalEarth) superadobe technology, which uses sandbags, barbed wire, and earth to create structures that are resistant to earthquake, fire, and flood.

Upon arriving at the hospital, Dr. Appel quickly looked over the baby. He appeared healthy. There was a poorly done X-ray, and the malaria smear, collected at the Regional Medical Center, was positive. His family had left the Regional Medical Center against medical advice, making the long, twelve-mile trek through the bush to bring their baby to the Baraka Adventist Hospital, founded by Adventist Health International (AHI). AHI is a nonprofit corporation focused on upgrading and managing Seventh-day Adventist-affiliated mission hospitals throughout Africa, Asia, and the Americas by providing governance, consultation, and technical assistance.

The Baraka Adventist Hospital had opened in May 2017 with a mission to address the desperate health-care situation in eastern Chad. Led by a local Adventist physician, Dr. Tirmon Kjakissam, and Chadian staff, the hospital was soon swamped and needed to add a second full-time physician, Dr. Mbusa Carockey. Dr. Appel worked part-time as a consultant.

After Dr. Appel finished examining the baby, he decided that surgery could wait for the morning. He tried to text the operating room team to warn them to be ready early the following day, but the network was down. Giving final instructions to the hospital staff, he returned home to his bed. However, sleep was elusive, chased away by thoughts of operating on a five-day-old baby in the morning.

When dawn finally broke, he texted the nurse anesthetist, Daniel, and the scrub nurse, Service, who promised to come. At the wards, to his relief, the baby still looked well, his abdomen swollen but not tense, with stable vital signs and no fever.

While Service and Dr. Appel scrubbed for surgery, Daniel searched for a new IV because the first had gone bad. The pulse oximeter, an instrument that reads the saturation of oxygen in the blood, wasn't working.

"Better get the pediatric stethoscope and listen to his heart. His breathing looks shallow," warned Dr. Appel.

Dr. Appel put on his gown and gloves and then started the incision for the colostomy, a surgical procedure that would bring one end of the large intestine to exit through a surgically created hole in the abdominal wall. The blood in the surgical field was dark. He glanced at the child's lips, and they were blue.

"Daniel! Does he have a heartbeat?"

Daniel listened before replying, "No."

Immediately, Dr. Appel began chest compressions. "Get some oxygen on him! Keep listening with the stethoscope!"

The pulse oximeter, which was designed to be used on a finger, was adult-sized and simply too big for use on an infant, and there was no pediatric attachment.

"Don't we have a bag valve mask?" Dr. Appel asked. Having to adapt equipment to different uses was almost an everyday occurrence. Daniel scrambled to find one, and Dr. Appel struggled to use it. The mask was almost as big as the baby's head. Finally, the pulse oximeter started working, and the oxygen saturation began to rise. The baby's heart began to beat, and he started breathing on his own.

Once the baby was stable, Dr. Appel opened up the peritoneum, the membrane that forms the lining of the abdominal cavity. Bowel burst out. The colon, however, was so swollen it wouldn't come out, and he had to extend the incision until he could get his fingers inside to compress the colon and extricate it. He closed up the incision so that it was just big enough for the ostomy, an alternate exit the baby would need for stool to pass from his body. He opened the bowel. Stool and gas immediately began pouring out, and the suction couldn't keep up as stool spilled everywhere. Dr. Appel and Service mopped it up, and Daniel doused everything with diluted bleach as Dr. Appel finished the procedure.

Returning the baby to his mother on the ward, Dr. Appel began rounds while listening to the steady beep-beep of the pulse oximeter attached to the baby. He checked on two prostatectomy patients who were both doing well without bladder irrigation. Dr. Appel encouraged them to drink a lot, start eating, and walk around. The man with cirrhosis needed more liquid taken off his abdomen. Dr.

Appel poked a large needle in and let the fluid drip into a basin. He instructed Josué, one of the nurses, to keep an eye on it while he moved on. The man with a fracture of the kneecap from a gunshot wound that he had internally fixed with a wire was finally keeping his leg brace on. The exit wound on the side of his lower leg was starting to heal.

The old woman with a crushed forearm and old lower leg fracture that he had repaired was as sharp and funny as ever. Her spirits and courage were so good that she was healing quickly; many others wouldn't have been doing as well in the same situation. The baby with malaria and anemia had finished his blood transfusion and four days of IV quinine and was ready to go home. The woman with the chest tube hadn't had much drainage for three days. Dr. Appel put some bacitracin ointment on a gauze pad, cut the suture holding the chest tube in place, and yanked it out as she breathed in deeply. He then put pressure on the hole with the gauze and ointment.

Rounds finished, Dr. Appel headed home.

Over the next several days, the health of the baby with the colostomy went up and down like a roller coaster. One moment he was breastfeeding, then the next, he was unconscious. Later, he was stable with no fever, then his heart rate slowed down and his oxygen levels dropped. Every day, with every change of nursing shift, someone came to give Dr. Appel some more bad news about the child. But then the next day the baby would still be there doing fine. During the nights of fitful sleep, he prayed every time he woke up.

At last, the baby slipped into a coma and passed away.

Dr. Appel cautiously approached the baby, uncovered him, and listened to his heart with his stethoscope.

"He's in God's hands now," he encouraged the parents in broken Chadian Arabic.

The man and woman nodded. "*Al hamdullilah!* (Praise be to God!)" they replied.

Dr. Appel held out his hands, palms up. "*Al Fatiha.*" Again, the couple nodded and raised their hands up as well. Together, western physician and Muslim parents prayed in the name of God, praising Him as Lord of the worlds, Master of the day of judgment, the only One we praise and seek help from, and the One who can guide us onto the straight path.

As Dr. Appel put his palms to his face and down to his heart, the father reached out his hand, and they clasped wrists. His firm grip and the tears in his eyes told of the power of reconciliation.

"*Allah yabarrik fik!* (May God bless you!)"

And with that, Dr. Appel moved on to the next patient on what seemed like endless hospital rounds.

*"Blessed are the peacemakers,
for they will all be called children of God."*

—Matthew 5:9, NIV

A Better Way

The Center for Conflict Resolution at La Sierra University

Debbie Pershing was dismayed as she watched the little drama play out in her kindergarten classroom at La Sierra Academy in Riverside, California.

Bianca approached her best friend Allyson and asked, "Where should we sit?"

"I'm sitting with Riana today," Allyson replied. "And if you try to sit with us, I'm not inviting you to my birthday party."

Pershing had just started teaching kindergarten but had seen issues such as these arise with her fifth-graders for years. Despite her years of teaching, continuing education, and a graduate degree, she had never received training on how best to address what she had just witnessed.

When discussing this incident with other educators and adults, Pershing found their responses ranged from the credible to the absurd.

"It's just kids being kids."

"It's bad parenting."

"Teachers shouldn't put their noses into the kids' social lives."

"Teachers have no right to say who should be friends."

"It's a sign that Bible isn't being taught."

"If you intervene, you are just teaching the kids to be victims."

"Students need to learn that sticks and stones may break bones, but words will never hurt them."

None of those answers satisfied, and none seemed to have a clear understanding of what was taking place between the two little girls whose situation was made more bizarre because not only were they best friends, their families had been friends for years and frequently went on outings together.

Time passed, and the question of how to handle situations of that kind kept nagging at Pershing.

In 2010, La Sierra University in Riverside, California, opened the Center for Conflict Resolution in the Tom and Vi Zapara School of Business. In its quest for an evidence-based approach to use in the kindergarten through grade-twelve school setting, the center found the work of Scandinavian researcher Dan Olweus, PhD, and his American counterpart, Susan Limber, PhD, at Clemson University in Northern Carolina. Olweus had pioneered work in the field of student relationships, specifically, peer abuse, or as it is commonly known, bullying. He had commenced this work long before it had come to the attention of the media in the United States. The importance of his research first became known in 1983 when three school-age suicides in Norway spurred the country's leadership to make bullying prevention a national priority.

All three suicides in Norway were linked to patterns of bullying behavior. Norway's education leadership asked Olweus to help them develop an approach that would reduce bullying behavior in schools and, in its place, develop a culture of kindness. Olweus conducted further research in Norway and helped the country become the first nation to implement what is now known as the Olweus Bullying Prevention Program (OBPP).

The most startling discovery of the OBPP resulted when Olweus compared the statistical information of the large metropolitan schools with the one-room schools out in the rural areas of the country. There was no statistical difference between the rate of bullying between the two types of schools. In fact, there was a slightly higher amount of bullying in the small schools, but it was not "statistically significant."

The other discovery of the OBPP that surprised the center had to do with the distinction between conflict process and abuse process. While conflict resolution processes worked well for the resolution of actual conflicts between disputants with relatively equal bargaining power, bullying is peer abuse. Abuse processes are about the exercise of power over another person in a harmful way, not about conflicting views on a particular topic.

In 2012 some six thousand Adventist educators convened in Nashville, Tennessee, for the North American Division Teacher's Convention. Pershing volunteered to attend the OBPP training and then be available to train others in Nashville. Not knowing what to expect, she boarded a plane for North Carolina, the only location where OBPP training was available before the convention.

When she entered a room filled with public school superintendents and principals from all over the United States, she was the only person representing private schools and, in particular, private Christian schools. *Maybe this OBPP isn't for small Christian schools like ours*, she thought.

Jane Riese, the OBPP national training director from Clemson University, rose to start the three days of training. As Pershing listened, she suddenly began to understand the behaviors she had been witnessing, such as the incident between the best friends. The initial anxiety of wondering whether the OBPP would be something that would benefit small Christian schools faded away, replaced by wonder as she absorbed a new understanding of a very old problem.

The training in North Carolina ended just a few weeks before the teacher's convention convened. Larry Blackmer, vice president for education for the North American Division of the Seventh-day Adventist Church, arranged for the center to have some break-out sessions at the conference. Pershing and other members of the center team conducted those presentations, ending each session with an offer to fund the implementation of the OBPP, hoping that at least one school would be willing to try out the program.

Kim Thompson, associate superintendent for the Georgia-Cumberland Conference, whose school had just lost a student who had been picked on, attended Pershing's training and with growing excitement realized that the approach was new and different and that it just might work. Returning home, she organized training for two schools in hopes of implementing the program. At first, the schools' team members were skeptical, but as the day progressed, they began to realize that the OBPP was not just another curriculum for them to master. Rather, it was a way for an entire school to work together on developing a culture of kindness with concerted efforts for intervening in negative behaviors.

Both schools had surveyed their students with the Olweus Bullying Questionnaire. The students' willingness to report on what behaviors were troubling them surprised the team leaders. The good news for both teams came from the students' report regarding how much they liked their school, well above the national comparison. Both teams appreciated having a way to assess annually what was happening in the relations between the students and what actions the schools could take to improve those relationships.

Since the launch of OBPP, the center has helped more than one hundred schools, churches, summer camps, and Pathfinder clubs in North America participate in the OBPP training. Trainers from the center are accustomed to a wide range of reactions from trainees. Sometimes the negative reactions stem from a fear of having more duties heaped on an already overworked team. This fear is well founded, considering the tremendous load teachers in small schools carry. They often work all week and then help with Pathfinders and church youth and children's events on the weekends. This reaction is assuaged, however, as they learn that the OBPP will reduce their burden, not increase it.

On April 18, 2002, the General Conference of the Seventh-day Adventist Church issued an official call for peace. The Seventh-day Adventist Church operates what may be the second largest worldwide parochial school system. The statement asked that each of its more than six thousand schools, colleges, and universities "set aside one week each school year to emphasize and highlight, through various programs, respect, cultural awareness, nonviolence, peacemaking, conflict resolution, and reconciliation as a way of making a specifically 'Adventist' contribution to a culture of social harmony and peace."

The "Call for Peace" statement additionally commented that "while peacemaking may seem to be a forbidding task, there is the promise and possibility of transformation through renewal. All violence and terrorism are really one aspect of the ongoing controversy, in theological terms, between Christ and Satan. The Christian has hope because of the assurance that evil—the mystery of iniquity—will run its course and be conquered by the Prince of Peace and the world will be made new."

It is the Center for Conflict Resolution's mission to help the denomination achieve these objectives. One of its most important contributions has been to bring the Olweus Bullying Prevention Program to denominational schools throughout the North American Division.

Hope's Mission

Mamawi Atosketan Native School

When Hope was a sixteen-year-old high school student, she got into trouble with the law in the city of Edmonton in the province of Alberta, Canada. She had gone out drinking with friends, and she intentionally broke the side mirror off the door of a parked car. She walked by the car and just knocked off the mirror. It was a small offense, but it was still a crime. Everyone agreed that Hope needed to be punished, but how?

A restorative justice officer—a law enforcement officer who works with indigenous young people in Canada—called Hope's father to attend a meeting to discuss the punishment. Her father, in turn, called Hope's principal at Mamawi Atosketan Native School (MANS), Canada's only Seventh-day Adventist mission school.

MANS is an accredited, nonfunded private school, as defined by the Alberta Ministry of Education. Its staff is 24 percent First Nations and has an average tenure of eight years. MANS serves the four Cree bands of Maskwacis, educating approximately two hundred reserve students from kindergarten to grade twelve with an enriched program that is culturally sensitive and tailored to the realities of reserve life. A residential school model is not an option in Canada. Historically, residential schools are synonymous with the forced removal of children as young as five from their families and terrible abuse in church-run boarding schools. In 2014, Canada concluded its Truth and Reconciliation Commission for residential school survivors and paid millions in reparations. The MANS model allows the school to work with families in addition to children and youth, and the school is well-respected in the reserve community because of this.

The Chiefs Assembly on Education (a Canadian assembly) found that a First Nations youth in Canada is more likely to go to jail than to graduate from high school. Fewer than 40 percent of those who register for high school graduate. If MANS intervened during this critical time, it could change lives and, eventually, communities.

"Can you please come to the meeting?" Hope's father asked the principal. "I want someone who can say something good about Hope. I don't want it all to

Hope's Mission

Mamawi Atosketan Native School students pass out blankets at a reserve near the First Nations camp meeting in Port Hardy, BC

be bad just because she made a mistake." The principal, Gail Wilton, and school guidance counselor agreed to attend the meeting on the First Nations reserve where Hope and her father lived.

At the meeting, the adults talked about how Hope could be punished without having to go to court and maybe jail. Her father made arrangements to pay for the broken mirror. Then the adults looked to the school principal. What could the school do to help Hope?

Gail thought for a moment, praying God would give her inspiration. She said, "The school will help Hope write a letter of apology to the owner of the car. And we'll give Hope the chance to do something to help others."

Before the school even had time to consider a way for Hope to help others, she came up with an idea of her own. She wanted to collect fluffy, warm blankets to give away to people who needed them on her reserve. She told her plan to one of her classmates.

"Where are you going to get the blankets?" the classmate asked.

"I don't know," Hope said. "I haven't thought that far ahead yet."

The classmate liked the idea very much, and she had an idea of her own. She said, "For every weekend that you don't go out drinking, I will donate one blanket to your project."

Then her classmate shared the blanket idea with the school's teachers, and they wanted to participate, too. The teachers said, "For every weekend that Hope does not go out drinking, we will donate blankets as well."

On Monday morning, Hope arrived at school and announced that she hadn't had a drink all weekend. Her classmate and each of the teachers gave her a blanket.

The next Monday, the same thing happened again. The blankets began to flow in.

Supporters donated so many blankets to Hope that the local store owner asked, "What's going on? I keep running out of blankets at the store!"

When he found out about Hope's project, he also wanted to get involved. He ordered extra blankets and began to donate them.

Soon a classroom was filling with blankets, and the principal decided it was time to begin giving them away. She looked through the school's list of students to see which families were the most in need, and then a teacher drove Hope to the reserve with the blankets. She saw many happy smiles and heard many thanks as she handed out the blankets. The project was such a success that Hope gave it a name: Hope's Mission.

A big moment for Hope's Mission came in the spring when teachers took Hope and several other students on a ten-day trip to a special camp meeting for First Nations in Port Hardy, British Columbia. For many, it was their first trip off the reserve. Between the meetings, Hope and her friends passed out blankets at a nearby reserve.

One of Hope's friends who recently graduated singled out that experience as the best thing that happened in all her years at MANS. It was a student initiative for the community, and they were rewarded in many ways: travel, community admiration, and a sense of accomplishing something significant together, all because Hope redirected her focus to others. In the process, she made her own life and future more hopeful as well.

Grandma "Jonah"

ASAP Ministries

Grandma Kongsri had been dreaming, and the dream was a bad one. When she woke in the morning, she felt an urgency to get up and get ready. She had a busy morning ahead of her, but first, she had to drive her granddaughter Ruth to school on her motorcycle. She had raised her children to know God, and now she was raising her granddaughter as well. After she deposited Ruth safely at school, there were visits to be made to new church members. Grandma Kongsri takes care of three church groups and conducts seven Bible studies every week in addition to raising eight-year-old Ruth. She stays very busy indeed.

Grandma Kongsri is employed as a church planter in Thailand by ASAP (Advocates for Southeast Asians and the Persecuted) Ministries, which partners with Thailand Adventist Mission. ASAP provides yearly training for Grandma Kongsri and also has a field supervisor who visits her to encourage, support, help identify the needs of, and evaluate her church plant with additional training provided by Thailand Adventist Mission. Grandma Kongsri is a faithful worker who loves the Lord and has a special burden for young people.

But now, as she helped Ruth prepare for school, she couldn't shake the memory of her dream. In the night, she had heard a voice saying, "I want you to go to Noy Noy village to share My love. I have someone waiting there for you."

Grandma Kongsri frowned and shook her head firmly side to side. *Anywhere but Noy Noy village*, she thought.

"No," she said aloud while she cooked her breakfast and made plans for her day. "I won't be going there. That's a bad village. A very, very bad village. I have church members and new interests who need me. I know where I must visit. And that bad place is not on my list. Besides," she reasoned, "who would I talk to there anyway? I don't know a soul in that village. It was just a bad dream. That is all. I won't think about it anymore."

After she dropped Ruth off at school, Grandma Kongsri realized she had forgotten her bag, the one that contained her Bible, so she headed back home. On the way, the persistent, unwelcome thought came again: *I want you to go to Noy*

Grandma "Jonah" Kongsri, left, is a church planter in Thailand for ASAP Ministries.

Noy village. I have someone waiting.

Grandma Kongsri tried to push the thought out of her mind again. Everybody in that village was a castaway. Prostitutes and druggies, all of them. *I don't want to go there*, she thought. She drove the motorcycle faster. *I had better hurry. I'm almost late for my appointment.*

Back at the house, she tried to push her key into the heavy lock. It wouldn't go in. "I've never had this problem before," she muttered and tried harder. It wouldn't budge. She started to get angry. "I'm going to break this lock or kick the door down!" Gentle Grandma Kongsri was unusually upset, and this gave her pause. Suddenly she felt rebuked in her spirit, and she knew immediately why she was angry with something as inconsequential as a lock.

"Am I being a Jonah? Am I trying to run away from God? Am I mad at the lock like Jonah was mad at the worm?" She stopped struggling and surrendered. She did not want to go to Noy Noy village, but neither did she want to run from the Lord. She thought of the reluctant prophet and relented in her heart. If Noy Noy village was her Nineveh, she would go. She would not run in the opposite direction. But she definitely didn't *want* to go there.

She bowed her head. "Lord, make me willing to go," she prayed.

She decided to try the lock once more. The key slipped in easily as always. Grabbing her Bible, she raced down the street on her motorcycle, but this time she was not headed to a church member's house. She drove straight toward Noy Noy village.

"But what will I say when I get there?" she asked God. Nothing came to her mind; it was blank. She didn't know anyone, and she didn't know what to say. As she drew closer to the village, her dread increased. "Lord, give me the words to speak and someone to speak them to."

When she pulled into the town, her eyes opened wide in surprise. Right there was a school friend she had not seen since her childhood! Excitedly they began to talk, sitting in the shade beneath her friend's house. They chatted about their school days and caught each other up on their lives.

"Ah, yes," said the friend teasingly. "I remember how you, Kongsri, used to steal fruit from the neighbor's trees. You weren't content to share them with your friends, either. You made us buy them from you!"

They laughed, then Grandma Kongsri began to tell her friend how she had met Jesus and how His love had changed her heart. As Grandma Kongsri shared her testimony, four of those "bad" village girls pressed in to listen. Grandma Kongsri smiled and told them stories of God's love. It was the beginning of a new ministry in a new town, because Grandma "Jonah" had stopped running from God's voice.

We must all do what we can for others, she realized as she was driving back home on her motorcycle. *We all have a part to play.* This realization was confirmed to her one night, not long after, when little Ruth saw her wincing as she picked up something heavy.

"Grandma Kongsri, what's wrong with your wrist? It's pokey and bumpy." The little girl touched the sore, swollen place on Grandma Kongsri's wrist.

"I need to have surgery," Grandma Kongsri answered. "But it's expensive, and I'm scared."

"I'll pray for you," offered little Ruth. "Jesus can do anything." She rubbed the soft, wrinkled wrist while she prayed.

The next day, Grandma Kongsri lifted the heavy pail again, expecting the sharp pain. She felt nothing. Looking down, she was startled to see her wrist was as smooth as the uninjured one. There was no doubt that God loved her—and little Ruth and her church members and all the people in Noy Noy village too.

Move Over, Mountain

Youth and Family Life Education Institute

To Sandra Hawkins, a public-school educator, the needs of the youth she taught were deep, and their needs were many. They needed a voice. They needed help. Somebody had to step up. It was becoming increasingly clear to her that she was the someone God had in mind. In 2000, she founded Youth and Family Life Education Institute (YFLEI) and began helping the residents of Montgomery, Alabama, serving the inner city and surrounding areas.

One day she noticed one of her fifth-grade girls, Monique,* wearing heavily applied lipstick to school every day. She also noticed the girl's hair needed a good, caring hand. She knew Monique's grandmother was looking after her and her little brother because their mother was in prison.

"Monique is going to tell you a story about what her older uncle did to her," other teachers warned Sandra. "She has a habit of lying. The story's just not true."

Sandra knew that a student's reputation, good or bad, often followed them from grade to grade or school to school. During the two years Monique was in Sandra's classroom, she got to know the family. Eventually, Monique did tell her teacher the story. Sandra believed her and reported it to school officials.

"Do you want those children taken from their grandmother and placed in foster care?" other teachers asked her. "That's what's going to happen," they warned. "And she has been untruthful about other things."

Sandra knew that likely meant Monique had not been silent and that school personnel knew her story; however, nothing was being done about it. She made home visits and spoke with Monique's grandmother very frankly and passionately. She met a young cousin and the older uncle in question and had very serious conversations with them concerning the issue.

Monique began to blossom in class. Sandra persisted, making frequent visits to her home to see that she received the attention to her personal needs that she knew every young girl should receive. Her efforts were rewarded and made an astounding difference in Monique's life. In part, she credited the grandmother's

---

* Not her real name.

willingness to grant her permission to be involved in Monique's life and to become her advocate, to be sure that she was clothed, attended school, had social interaction, and wasn't hungry. Sandra became the person she could confide in who was also allowed to monitor her and be sure that home situations affecting her negatively were addressed and rectified. She took the younger brother under her wing as well.

Sandra believed the traumatic event going on in Monique's life had stopped because her student arrived at school much happier. She began participating, and her peers started to accept her. She stopped wearing the bright red band of lipstick around her mouth. Her personality, long buried beneath the trauma of what was happening in her life, developed and began to shine. Monique, whom Sandra had practically adopted in her classroom, had blossomed, and Sandra was feeling really good about the intervention.

Sandra began seeing other ways she could help the community. One critical need was for technology. In wealthier parts of town, children and adults could easily come to community centers to do research projects or entertain themselves if they chose not to use their home computers. Not so with Sandra's students, who had no home computers and no community place to access the Internet. The digital divide stared back at her every day when she walked into her classroom.

Bethany Christian Academy, a local Seventh-day Adventist school, could not afford to purchase and set up a technology center, but Sandra knew that a technology lab in the building would service Bethany students during the school year and community children during the summer months. In addition to bridging the technology gap in the community, a lab would provide a bridge between Bethany Christian Academy and the community surrounding the school.

YFLEI helped obtain grants, and Bethany Christian Academy opened a technology center. They even had enough funds remaining to hire a technology teacher for summer classes. Sandra was gratified to see Monique and her brother among the students who attended the very first class. Bethany's lab was the third Community Technology Assistance Project that YFLEI had established.

At the nearby Houston Hills Community Center, Sandra saw a desperate need to help the center serve children and senior citizens in the community. She asked the director what YFLEI could do to help, and he explained their needs. He gave her a tour, pointing out the leaking roof the city refused for years to fix. He showed her the missing and broken ceiling tiles in the main gathering area. On rainy summer days, during lunch, staff positioned the children strategically to keep raindrops from falling into their food. These children weren't from the affluent side of town or even the middle-class areas. They were children from the housing projects whose most nutritious meal of the day was often the government lunch the community center provided when school was out for the summer.

The restrooms horrified Sandra. Crusty, rusty, dank, and poorly lit, the restrooms were places she would never have let her own children *enter*, much less *use*.

Two of the main rooms upstairs had no working air conditioner, which made the space intolerable during Montgomery's hot summers. Sandra knew she needed to help the community center.

"You'll never do it," said city officials, community residents, and even the people working at the community center. "This building has been in sad shape for years. The city won't do anything, and no one is interested in putting money into a place where kids have no sense of value. We've already tried."

However, this inner-city missionary knew from experience that what God ordained, He sustained. She began to advocate strongly for the community center, and in time, the city provided both funding and labor for a new roof, new ceiling tiles, and new air conditioners. Grants funded new computers, and the community center refurbished a room for student use after school. YLFEI helped supply arts and crafts materials for the many students who attended the community center for summer childcare. The organization also helped equip the center for activities and shared the children's field trip expenses. Recognizing the need for children to showcase their work, YFLEI sponsored a community art show. With determined persistence and combined city labor and grant funding, they transformed the community center into a place that could welcome children with more dignity.

Sandra sees the continued leading of God in every project YFLEI undertakes. She believes that you must always *over*estimate the power of prayer, faith, and hard work. When God says yes, He means yes and expects us to keep moving right on past the naysayers because they don't have the last word. With God, mountains can be moved.

The Peaceful Path

The Center for Conflict Resolution at La Sierra University

In 2010, Robin Burke's connection in Phoenix was late, and the plane was held for her. She boarded in a rush, looking around for a place to sit. All the other passengers had already filled the plane, and there were very few open seats. Robin quickly realized that, of course, all of them were middle seats. She approached a gentleman who was studiously avoiding eye contact with her.

"Excuse me," Robin said, preparing to take the seat next to him. "Can I sit here?"

"Of course."

Tony Belak, an instructor at the Center for Conflict Resolution at La Sierra University, was flying from Ontario back to Louisville after conducting a basic skills training in mediation.

As they began talking, Tony and Robin found they were kindred spirits. The long flight seemed to last mere minutes as they talked and found their common ground. Tony explained the mediation process to Robin, which interested her very much, and his words resonated with what she needed. Tony asked her to join the next class in a few weeks, and she accepted his offer. As it turned out, that class had a dramatic and positive impact on her life.

Professionally, Robin was a documentary filmmaker and consultant for a variety of nonprofit organizations. Her work was mostly project-driven. The projects were intensive and could extend anywhere from two months to four or five years, often with people who had never worked together before and in unfamiliar locations.

In both settings, production and the built environment, it seemed to her that three things happened that were essential for success and a joyful attitude: collaboration; class, race, and age intersection; and communication. In her role as producer, she loved to pay attention to what was happening on those fronts. They were the nuances of relationship building. Also, she knew the goal was typically communal. Many interactions occurred, which created many opportunities for creativity, interpretation, misunderstanding, and—conflict. Discovering a practical discipline—mediation—that complemented her professional life was exciting, and Robin attended the basic training with eagerness.

Her classmates were terrific and hailed from many different walks of life. Some were oriented from a business perspective, others from social services, law, education, hospitality, and diplomacy. Everyone was fully engaged and shared their process and networks generously. The instruction was dynamic. Tony Belak, assisted by Sue Hamilton and several guest presenters, shared an enormous amount of information and material. Besides the reading and case studies, there were group discussions, role-play, and diagramming. Robin's imagination found it akin to scripting and storyboarding. She knew it was something she could apply in everyday life; it was naturally familiar.

Her biggest takeaway from the basic mediation class was learning that a person could be "a neutral." This concept blew her mind. She had never heard of that before. What did it mean to be a neutral? *Neutral* as a noun. To maintain neutrality? To react to disputes and conflict with neutrality? How was it practiced?

Another realization came when, in class, they examined the fact that conflicts exist everywhere and often. Learning this had a very calming effect on Robin. She decided to delve deeper into the broader field of conflict transformation.

Robin was accepted to Eastern Mennonite University's Summer Peacebuilding Institute in Harrisonburg, Virginia, and studied with the "grandfather of restorative justice" Howard Zehr and filmmaker and co-instructor Paulette Moore, among others. Again, she embraced the new opportunity to explore the fields of peace-building, restorative justice, emotional intelligence, compassion, art in conflict transformation, trauma awareness, playback theater, personal narrative, mapping, emotional intelligence, and collaborative workplace models.

She realized that she had a heartfelt desire to find peace and hope with others.

It had always been natural for Robin to try to bring groups to consensus and understanding. But often she had knee-jerk reactions—learned behaviors that were not attentive or kind and, as such, not particularly helpful. The basic mediation training offered ways for her to pay attention, remain neutral, acknowledge what motivated people, and bring tools to the conversation that would transform the conflict and resolve the problem satisfactorily while caring for individuals and the collective good.

Soon after the Center for Conflict Resolution opened its doors, providing the foundation for her personal shift, Restorative Justice Louisville opened as an alternative to the criminal justice system for first-time juvenile offenders. Robin trained and certified as a Restorative Justice facilitator. The formalities and distinct stages of the mediation process sought results that were very similar to the restorative justice process. Bringing the mediation training to her community grew her appreciation for the broadening network of facilitators and the multitude of applications for the techniques.

In 2014, Drepung Gomang Center for Engaging Compassion, based in

Louisville, Kentucky, undertook a massive project. "Youth Engaging Compassion: A Dialogue with the Dalai Lama" was a year-long, community-wide effort with thousands of youth and educators engaging in acts of kindness, thoughtful reflection, curriculum development, and compassion awareness, all in preparation for a far-reaching and intimate dialog with the Dalai Lama on stage at the Kentucky Center for the Performing Arts. They worked in committees with multiple stakeholders to unravel a myriad of program and production layers. Whenever problems or disputes arose, Robin found herself assuming a neutral role and focusing on solutions that were mutually beneficial and trusted. She believed that this served the complexity and importance of the project while helping to create and support the collective imagination.

Over time, the practice of mediation started influencing larger organizational support systems. The mediators, neutrals, and facilitators were more intentional about offering solutions that were purposefully healing, didn't instigate or agitate suffering, and helped to correct systemic problems. They found that the core mediation tenets of respect and deep listening, and the stages of conference facilitation, were transferable to many other situations, as well.

More recently, Robin was contracted to direct the collaboration of architects, planners, developers, city agencies, students, and volunteers to improve an underserved neighborhood streetscape. She coordinated seventeen major projects. Egos, varying interests, policy, historical harms, fear, gossip, and hearsay all found their way to the table at different times. Several people had basic mediation training, and they consciously encouraged all parties to work cooperatively to find solutions. They built consensus by mirroring and adapting their mediation training to the process.

Since that fateful flight, Tony Belak has continued to guide and mentor Robin. They have co-facilitated a variety of conferences, trainings, circles, mediations, and difficult conversations. Robin applied what she learned with film crews, construction crews, YouthBuild Louisville staff and students, the Mohammad Ali Center, Bellwood Home for Children, businesses, and families. She describes the process as a beautiful ride and credits it for the dramatic impact it's had on how she works with others.

Who could have predicted that the middle seat on an otherwise unremarkable flight would lead to so many peaceful resolutions?

*"Blessed are those who are
persecuted because of righteousness,
for theirs is the kingdom of heaven."*

—Matthew 5:10, NIV

Unshakable

Cuba Adventist Theological Seminary

When Orlando Leyva del Toro learned that he had to go through the prescribed military service in Cuba, he was stunned. Generally, young men between eighteen and twenty years old were required to go through military service, but since he was already twenty-two, he had assumed he wouldn't be called. At the time, he was studying for a career in psychology. As a Seventh-day Adventist, it was proving a difficult degree to pursue due to his absence from Saturday classes to observe Sabbath.

He was excited to study for such a good career—one that he enjoyed and wanted to practice. But when he received the appointment to military service, he had to put his budding career on hold for two years. The military authorities promised him that once he had completed his service period, he could reintegrate himself into his career without any difficulty. He explained to the military men who interviewed him that he was a Seventh-day Adventist, but they paid little attention.

They sent him first to a training facility in the province of Bayamo. Orlando notified the first lieutenant, who was his immediate boss, about his Sabbath observance as well as his refusal to take up arms due to his religious beliefs.

"I'll need to request authorization from your pastor," the first lieutenant informed him.

"It's not a matter for my pastor," Orlando argued. "It's an issue of my conviction as a Christian."

"Your pastor is going to have problems with the authorities," the first lieutenant observed with a scowl. "He's putting ideas into young people's heads that run contrary to the laws of the country."

When the first Sabbath arrived, Orlando separated himself from the squad, taking his pocket Bible so that he could study and pray a little. This action earned him the label of "deserter."

The lieutenant arrived shortly, bringing with him the military man in charge of political affairs. He glared at Orlando.

"You deserve to be punished for this insubordination," he said angrily.

"I'm sorry, sir, but I cannot show up for duty on this Sabbath or any other," Orlando replied firmly.

"Who sent you here?" the lieutenant demanded. "What are you doing in this unit?"

"With all due respect, Lieutenant, I am asking myself that same question," replied Orlando. "Why don't you release me, and we won't have any problems?"

The lieutenant waved one hand dismissively. "That is no longer possible. You are already on the list of new recruits."

Each day, a different officer interviewed Orlando and advised him to take up arms and to follow orders on Sabbath. They threatened that if he did not do so, he would be detained, and he would lose his psychology career. Orlando's response remained unshakable. If that was what they had to do, he would face it. Whatever happened, it would not alter his thinking or his actions.

Eventually, Orlando's superior officers took him to the highest-ranking colonel of the unit, who, with the foulest and most offensive language that Orlando had ever heard, yelled at Orlando, pounding on the table and accusing him of being a lazy coward.

"What would happen to this country if everyone thought as you do?" the colonel screamed.

Orlando, praying to God in silence and asking Him for wisdom, responded, "Then we would have peace."

The colonel changed tack. "And what would happen if they came to kill your family and you had a weapon by your side? Would you allow your loved ones to be killed?"

"I have never been in a similar situation," Orlando replied. "But I'm sure there would be something I could do that would not be contrary to the will of God."

The colonel forbade Orlando to read his Bible, but Orlando never turned it over to his superiors and read it discreetly. Drill sergeants challenged him physically, but God helped him grow in patience, which was one of the main battles he needed to win to be a better Christian. The day before he was due to pledge allegiance to the flag, which he believed would imply swearing an oath of loyalty and obedience to the army, he refused to do so while in formation as the drills were in progress.

A new lieutenant took Orlando out of formation and spoke with him.

"Look, Seven," he said, calling Orlando not by his name but by his number. "I want to help you, but you are refusing everything. How about this: tomorrow, you can fire a single shot, and I'll grade you as though you had completed the entire maneuver."

Orlando refused, reasoning that firing once would have been the same as firing one hundred times, since he would be violating his principles, the very ones he had defended up to that point.

Peers and superiors accused him daily of not being brave enough; the unit chief harangued him to take up arms since he was there to learn to kill. The assembly and breaking down of a weapon would have been a minor issue, but yielding to these demands by violating his principles and preparing himself to kill, as they insisted he do, was not part of his plan, nor was it part of God's plan for him.

On the morning he was supposed to pledge allegiance, superiors again told Orlando that it was his last opportunity to change his mind; otherwise, everyone else would receive a pass to go home, and he would remain detained and not be allowed any visitors.

Once again, Orlando told them, "I cannot fail God, no matter what you need to do."

A few minutes before the ceremony was to begin, the lieutenant arrived, dressed in civilian clothes. Dressed as he was, he could not participate in the ceremony. He went to the barracks and asked Orlando for his uniform. He affixed his rank and his stripes and informed Orlando that he did not need to show up to the ceremony. He instructed him to take care of the entire barracks and dress as a civilian. Orlando marveled at how God had saved him from a dangerous situation.

At the end of his intensive training, Orlando was allowed to go home. He was able to maintain his position in spite of the threats and abuse. For the remainder of his military service, he was assigned to a work unit, where God was with him every second, prospering him and blessing him. Before the required two years had ended, he was discharged with a commendation for his unimpeachable conduct. His fellow soldiers and his immediate military superiors said that he was truly a Christian because he had not violated his beliefs and principles.

In the end, Orlando was not able to continue his psychology career, despite promises that he would be able to renew his university studies after his military service. The only explanation he received was that the school did not offer his course of study that year. However, he enjoyed his increasing responsibilities at the church he attended, so he decided to apply for admission to the Adventist Theological Seminary in Cuba. He failed the English test, and school officials advised him to try again the next year. In the meantime, he organized five small groups, resulting in thirty-three baptisms in ten months.

The following year, the seminary accepted Orlando's application. The next four years were difficult; he got married and had to balance his studies and work. Several times he didn't have money to pay the rent, but the Lord provided every time. Following graduation, Orlando and his wife began working in several districts with churches and small groups. They firmly believe that the seminary in Cuba is vital in preparing people for the ministry by teaching and inspiring students with new knowledge and techniques for pastoral work.

The church is growing in Cuba and has more than forty thousand members. The seminary, which grants bachelor's degrees in theology to men and women every year, provides a much-needed workforce of pastors and Bible workers like Orlando, who are committed to spreading the gospel on the island.

Trial by Fire

Pine Springs Ranch

On a hot Monday afternoon in the middle of July 2013, staff and campers at Pine Springs Ranch could see a cloud of smoke as they walked out of the cafeteria after lunch. It was a little disconcerting, but the smoke seemed far enough away that it wasn't a threat. Smoke and even flames had been visible many times before, but never had a wildfire swept through the camp. Nevertheless, Carmen Ibañez, the camp director, and a few of her leadership staff, including Jeremy Cruz, David Machado, and Fritz Wuttke, drove up the dirt road to get a better view. At first glance, the fire did not appear to be a threat to Pine Springs Ranch. They were relieved that the fire was not close, but because a lot of smoke was drifting through camp, there was some concern for the campers. Ibañez and her team prayed together and discussed a strategy in case things got worse.

In the meantime, campers moved indoors because of the poor air quality. The staff closed open windows to prevent the smoke from getting inside. They also prepared to evacuate, just in case, and had their vehicle keys handy. Shortly after that, a sheriff stopped by to inform Ibañez that there was a voluntary evacuation order, but he didn't think the camp needed to evacuate at the moment. In spite of the officer's assurances, Ibañez, Cruz, Machado, and Wuttke were impressed that they should evacuate the camp.

They implemented the emergency evacuation plan, and the staff began with all the necessary procedures. Schools and churches stood by as potential evacuation sites for campers and staff, depending on which roads were still open. Then they updated the conference office in case worried parents began to call. Emails and texts went out to notify parents that their children were evacuating from camp. The staff packed medications, medical records, and files to transport with campers and staff. Then they counted cars to make sure there were enough seats for all 179 people—campers, volunteers, and staff. Next, the staff shut down propane and fuel tanks and electricity, and they verified that the water supply was available in case firefighters needed it. The staff who lived on-site quickly grabbed a few essentials, thinking they would be back at camp later that evening. Meanwhile, summer camp staff kept the campers entertained by playing games

Smoke from the 2013 mountain fire rises over Pine Springs Ranch.

in the main meeting room.

Machado, assistant director at Pine Springs Ranch, decided to stop by one of his favorite departments: horsemanship. When he walked up to the corral, he could see that the horses were agitated and scared because of the smoke. He knew that the horses' owner had instructed Ibañez to leave them in the hope that she could get them later. Machado talked to the horses for a little while and tried to soothe them. He told them that he had to go, but before he left, he prayed for them, asking God to protect and shield the horses from the oncoming fire.

Back at the emergency staging area, cars, vans, trucks, and a bus lined up, ready to be filled. One by one everyone boarded a vehicle that would take them to the safe evacuation site. Just as the cars were set to begin the drive, a highway patrol car drove up to the gate. Ibañez approached the vehicle.

"How quickly can you get out?" the officer asked. "There's no time to lose. The fire has traveled faster than anyone anticipated, and it's coming over the ridge."

Cruz led the caravan of vehicles out of the camp as Ibañez stood by the gate in disbelief, praying for God to stop the flames and protect the camp. She could hear the horses, and as she looked toward the corral, she saw them running back and forth in panic. It was such a heartbreaking scene that tears welled up in her eyes.

The last vehicle to leave included Ibañez, Machado, and Wuttke. Not one firefighter was in sight when they left. So many thoughts raced through their minds. They had originally believed that the fire was going to be contained well before it got to the camp, but now the flames were coming over the ridge right by the fort and the South Village camper cabins.

When the caravan arrived at the Hemet Seventh-day Adventist Church, some parents were already waiting to see their children. The church office staff was busy calling parents and contacting local businesses to help provide food for campers and staff. Several local businesses donated water, pizza, and snacks. Very quickly the church's gymnasium was overrun by energetic campers. The staff did an amazing job of keeping their attention by singing, playing games, and performing the scheduled nightly play. Several conference officers showed up to offer help.

That evening, Sandra Roberts, then executive secretary for the Southeastern

California Conference (elected its president in 2013) and a previous camp director, wanted to drive up to assess the situation at the camp. Roberts and Machado drove up the mountain as far as the fire officials and sheriff officers would let them. They stopped at the entrance of Hurkey Creek campground, just three miles from camp.

They were stunned.

The mountains surrounding Pine Springs Ranch glowed bright red with flames. They realized that the fire was more devastating than anyone had anticipated. They drove down the mountain in silence. When they arrived back at the church, Ibañez knew by the looks on their faces that the news was not good. They told her they didn't think the camp had made it.

The next morning Ibañez learned that she and Tim Rawson, the conference risk management director, might be allowed to go to the camp to look at the damage. They were going to go with an officer from the office of emergency services. Halfway up the road to camp, they came to an abrupt stop. Right in front of them, the fire jumped from one side of the road to the other. The officer said that they were going to have to wait a few minutes for the flames to calm down. Eventually, they arrived at the camp.

They drove slowly through the campground, surveying the fire's heartbreaking damage. The Wuttke's home, where they had lived for many years and had made so many family memories, had burned to the ground. The camp store, full of fun toys and awesome memories, was destroyed as if it had never existed. The old "post office" was gone. The maintenance shop and all of its contents had burned and melted beyond recognition. The wagons and one of the teepees had completely burned. The sewer plant's mechanical building was gone. The fort, where so many precious stories had been told, was gone. One of the three temporary staff cabins was gone. How could so much devastation have happened in less than twenty-four hours?

However, as Ibañez looked around, she was shocked to see how much *was* still standing: the cafeteria, the lodge, the nature center, all of the other staff homes, and so many other buildings remained. The boardwalk around Town Hall, the main office, had sustained damage, but it was still standing. Despite such huge losses, it was a miracle that God had spared so much of the camp. Ibañez wondered about the horses. How had they fared? The grass was blackened and scorched up to the very edge of the corral, but the horses were safe and sound. Ibañez was relieved and praised God for answering many of her prayers.

Pine Springs Ranch suffered major losses due to the fire; however, as many witnessed, God had His hand over the camp. After the fire, the camp closed for eight months. But God was in the midst of all the devastation, challenges, and rebuilding. What could have been a disastrous situation for so many campers and staff that day turned out to be a calm retreat in the midst of flames and destruction. God is good, and God is faithful. Because of His protection, Pine Springs Ranch continues to be a place of transformation.

The Tug of Truth

Hope Channel

Although Jacqueline had a good childhood, she was always sick. She had a health problem that made her constantly feel nauseated. Her mother, worried about her sickness, took her to visit her grandmother. During these visits, her grandmother acted differently and spoke in a voice that wasn't her own; it was not her grandmother's familiar voice at all. Jacqueline thought the visits were weird, but she didn't share her concerns with anyone.

Her father, on the other hand, would receive a spirit that said Jacqueline was a mean child. That spirit would torture her often. She was very little at the time and remembers feeling very bad and nasty whenever the spirit was around her. Whenever she felt she couldn't take the spirit's torture any longer, she had the same thought. She said, "Jesus, please take my life away right now. I'm in Your arms, and I can't take this torture any longer."

When she became a teenager, she started having greater conflicts with her dad because she did not agree with him about certain things. One Christmas Day, she didn't agree with what her dad was doing. At the time, she was standing at the end of a long hallway close to the kitchen in their house. Her dad was on the other end of the hall, close to the living room.

Suddenly, Jacqueline felt a cold chill run down her spine. Her father spoke to her mother, but his voice was not his own.

"Call the police right now," he said, "because our daughter is dead."

He began to run toward Jacqueline.

She stood her ground and said, "I'm not afraid of you because you have no power over me."

At that moment, her dad fell down like a dead man. She helped her mother and sister pick him up and carry him to the bed. His body was stiff and wouldn't move, just like a dead body. Everyone thought her father was dead, and Jacqueline began to feel guilty, thinking that she had killed him. It wasn't until years later that she would realize that even though she was living a sinful life away from the Lord, Jesus had still protected her. He had a plan for her life. There would come a time when she would see that it had been Jesus' hand freeing her from that dangerous situation.

The Tug of Truth

Jacqueline found Hope Channel on TV in Brazil, learned about Jesus' love, and accepted Him.

When she encountered the Hope Channel on TV in Brazil, Jacqueline did not know it was a religious station. She thought it was a local station. She and her husband watched it because there was no violence, the tone was always positive, and the news was different. One day she told her husband that they needed to start asking God to teach them His true religion.

In her prayers, she began to cry out to God, saying, "Lord, help me teach my kids about the God of Abraham, Isaac, and Jacob." It was a prayer she had learned from a movie that she had watched with her dad when she was a child.

Though she wasn't sure why, Jacqueline had always wanted a Bible, but she had never purchased one. Soon her husband got a new job. During his first day at work, when he opened the office drawers, he found a small Bible that contained the New Testament plus Psalms and Proverbs. He brought it home with him, and Jacqueline was very happy and excited that she finally had a Bible.

After reading Psalms and Proverbs, they began reading the book of Matthew—the first book in the New Testament. As they were studying and reading the Bible with their kids, they soon realized that Hope Channel was teaching about the Bible. It took them some time to make the connection.

One day, as Jacqueline was watching Hope Channel, Pastor Luís Gonçalves was teaching about the Bible.

"You have to watch this program," she told her husband. "This pastor talks about the Bible in a simple way, in a way that we can understand it! You know how sometimes when people try to explain things in the Bible, it sounds so complex, as if they are speaking in another language? When Pastor Gonçalves explains it, I can understand."

Jacqueline and her husband began to watch the program, and what the pastor said made sense to them. With only their small, incomplete Bible and the Hope Channel programs, their lives began to change.

When Jacqueline first started reading the Bible, she felt some negative spirits trying to move them away from the truth. So, she always asked the Lord to send His messengers to protect them. They believed in the Word of God and wanted to learn more about it. She truly believed that God was protecting them so that they could learn the truth.

It was a special moment when Jacqueline fully surrendered to the Lord the first time she attended church. She was sure the person sitting next to her must have thought she was a crazy woman. She cried the entire time she was at church. She cried through the praise service, through the prayers; she cried through every part of the service because she knew she wanted to give her life to Jesus. At the end of the church service, someone approached her offering Bible studies so that she could learn more about the Word of God.

"I want to be baptized," she answered promptly.

Looking back, she could see how Jesus rescued her from the deep mud and mire of her life to save her. Today, with Christ, she feels deep joy in her life. She has learned to trust God and knows that He is not far away and that He hears every one of her prayers. Jacqueline believes her life would still be hopeless if not for the Bible and the Hope Channel. Every day she praises God for the Hope Channel and for teaching her, guiding her, and helping her understand the Word of God.

Jacqueline's story is only one of many touched by the ministry of the Hope Channel. Every day, viewers make the life-changing journey from broadcast to baptism and beyond. As a result of evangelistic meetings broadcast nationwide in February and June 2018 by Hope Channel Tanzania, more than forty-three thousand people accepted Jesus and were baptized. In September, an evangelistic meeting in Lilongwe, Malawi, broadcast nationwide by Hope Channel Malawi, resulted in more than ten thousand baptisms.

Every day, lives are being transformed as a result of the Christ-centered, Bible-based programming on the Hope Channel networks.

Traffic Stop

Washington Adventist University Enactus

Enactus,* the largest entrepreneurial student organization around the world, is dedicated to creating a better world while developing the next generation of entrepreneurial leaders and social innovators. There are more than 460 Enactus teams on college and university campuses across the nation. In 2017, Enactus improved the lives of 1.3 million people through the work of 72,000 students spread across thirty-six countries.

Washington Adventist University (WAU), a small liberal arts university located in Takoma Park, Maryland, sponsors one of those 460 teams. Bordering the nation's capital, WAU has one of the most diverse communities in the nation, with a large number of Ethiopians, Hispanics, and other ethnic groups. In 2016, the Enactus team at WAU launched a new project titled "First Step, a Women Empowerment Program." The program was designed to assist Prince George's County's Langley Park women—especially those who had been victims of human trafficking or were vulnerable to grooming for that industry—with workforce skills and support.

Human trafficking is the act of using a person (of any age) without consent in order to make money (for labor, such as domestic servitude or for sex, such as forced prostitution). If a person is forced, defrauded, or coerced into a "job," it could be human trafficking. Some victims are kidnapped; most, such as runaways and immigrants, are groomed for months through friendship and the promise of a better life or high-paying job before being forced into slavery under threat of violence. (Voluntary sex workers are not considered victims of trafficking because they have the option to quit.)

Langley Park is more than 80 percent Hispanic, and that same percentage of the population speaks a non-English language. Only 42 percent are US citizens, and the poverty rate is 18 percent. Immigrants find it difficult to obtain meaningful employment due to low levels of education, the absence of real job

---

* *Enactus* is an acronym for the organization's motto: "We believe investing in students who take *en*trepreneurial *act*ion for others creates a better world for *us* all."

The 2016 WAU Enactus team launched an empowerment program for at-risk women in Prince George's County's Langley Park.

opportunities, high levels of poverty, and immigration problems.

To reduce the risk of grooming by traffickers, and to help those trapped in the situation to break free and assimilate into society, community members need training in computer skills, basic English, cultural orientation, and job preparation skills. Renee Battle-Brooks, assistant state's attorney for Prince George's County and an Adventist acquainted with one of the WAU Enactus team professors, asked whether the team would be willing to take on the project of helping the women. The team agreed, and university administrators approved the plan.

The university is located just two miles from where a lot of trafficking occurs. As part of a Christian university, the team considered it a moral obligation to meet this community need as far as possible. While they realized they could not eliminate the problem, they wanted to do something intentional to help. They worked in two phases. Phase one involved collecting relevant data on each person's need. Phase two included setting up training assistance.

Management at a nearby apartment complex renovated and leased the team a one-bedroom apartment equipped with phone and Internet to serve as a base of operations for the program, which launched in December 2016.

The team soon discovered that the situation was even more complex than they initially realized. From December 2016 to April 2017, just eight women asked for help with interviewing practice and other workforce skills. However, their visits were sporadic. The women had to be very careful about being seen with outsiders because the traffickers, or pimps, were often physically abusive to keep them in line.

Human trafficking has become the most common form of slavery all over the world. In the team's home state of Maryland, and in particular Prince George's

County, there has been a dramatic increase in trafficking because of its proximity to major transit routes, airports, and tourist venues. The latest available data showed that there were 396 survivors of human trafficking in Maryland that went through the state's trafficking task force (many more are yet unknown); 381 of those, more than half of them minor children, were victims of sex trafficking.

During the First Step program's early months, Hispanic immigrants were also warming to the idea of getting help with workplace preparation skills. However, as the new president's anti-immigrant political rhetoric escalated and Immigration and Customs Enforcement (ICE) began frequent sweeps, the women got scared and simply stopped coming. Most of them were undocumented, so they were very wary of strangers, and the threat of ICE capture and deportation left them distrustful.

In the fall of 2018, Enactus leaders arranged a consultative session with the manager of the apartments and discussed their challenge of reaching the potential clients. The manager told them that another agency, the Adelphi Judy Center, was meeting occasionally in the main building and was catering primarily to children. They decided that could be a great fit because, while the Adelphi Judy Center tended to the children, the Washington Adventist University Enactus team could assist the adults. The two organizations began working together out of the same apartment. The children come for tutoring while their parents get workforce training. In addition, a nearby business donates a bag of groceries weekly to each family.

The nearby Walmart store agreed to provide job opportunities to employable program clients. The trust factor is still an issue, and the trafficking issue is monumental, but the organizations continue to build relationships and provide help and hope for women who find themselves in a similar situation.

Rescued

ASAP Ministries

The district leader had stopped by to visit Diu.* The house church Diu attended in a closed country hadn't experienced much growth, and the district leader was visiting each member to encourage them to fast and pray for souls. The country Diu lived in ranked in the top twenty countries in the world where it is the most dangerous to follow Jesus. In 2018, it was listed in the very high persecution category in Open Doors's annual World Watch List, a reliable report on the persecution of Christians. The World Watch List is considered the most trusted measurement of persecution in the world today.

In Diu's communist country, church members encounter interrogations, fines, and harassment by the police if they are caught witnessing, so they are understandably hesitant to engage in active public evangelism. Even so, each Sabbath they bravely gather and pray for the Holy Spirit, for a love for people, and for courage to share their faith.

"The Lord will give you the courage to share the gospel, no matter what the consequences and risks," the district leader said. "It is up to us to carry the gospel to others. God will go with us."

The next Sabbath afternoon the church members blanketed an area with sermon DVDs. While the church members also pass out books and other literature, which are well-received, in Diu's country it is DVDs that have proven to be an effective method of sharing the gospel. A pastor produced more than two hundred of them, and they include sermons and music. The wide range of topics includes everything from how to have a happy family to understanding the beasts in Daniel.

Many people in that country have televisions and DVD players because a richer Asian country, which is its top donor, provided the country with televisions. The government requested this in order to spread their communist propaganda to the whole country through the television, which was a very effective way to do it. With the medium already in place, God used it to bring His good

---

* Name has been changed.

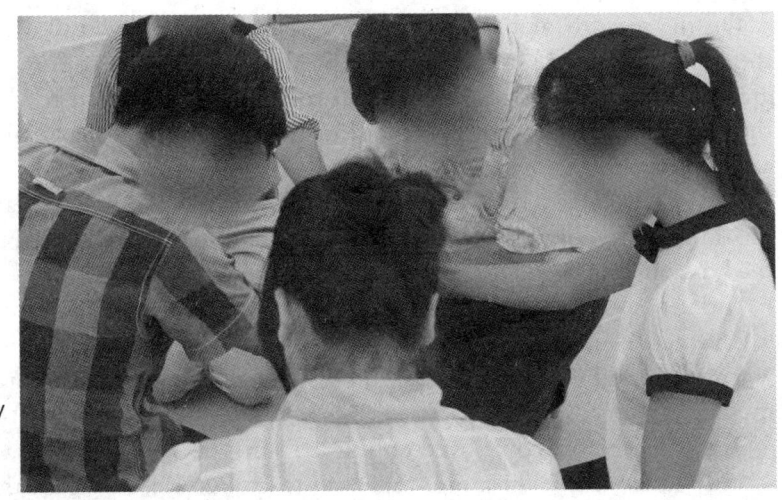

Christian believers in a closed country pray for the safe return of a kidnapped boy.

news to the people. Because many people enjoy watching a program rather than reading, the DVDs were well received.

DVDs have added benefits. They can deliver the message even to people who are illiterate. They are small and can be easily hidden in purses and backpacks. Videos can also be shared via website, Facebook, or flash drive.

When out witnessing one Sabbath, Diu stopped to talk to a lady selling meat beside the road. The lady asked, "Are you married?"

"No," Diu responded with a smile. "I'm still single, but I'm not alone. I'm so in love with Jesus that it feels like I'm married to Him in a way."

The lady was very surprised. No one had ever shared about Jesus with her before. Suddenly she burst into tears. Now it was Diu's turn to be surprised.

"What's wrong?" she asked tenderly, coming closer to her.

"It's my son, Tuan,"* the lady said between sobs. "He was seventeen when he disappeared two years ago, and I have no clue where he is or what happened to him. He was in the army, and I asked his sergeant and inquired all the way to the top commander, but no one has answers."

Because Diu's country is also one of the top ten countries in the world for rare minerals, they suspected he had been kidnapped for free labor in a gold mine. Human trafficking is a big problem in Southeast Asia. Diu sensed that this hopeless, heartbroken mother needed a miracle. She reassured her that she and the other church members would pray for her son.

They did exactly as she promised, coming together for fasting and united prayer. God heard and answered their earnest pleas because He loves rescue missions! This venture was not too hard for the One who sent His Son on the biggest rescue mission of all.

---

* Name has been changed.

On the seventh night of prayer, God sent an angel down to a dark room in the middle of a gold mine along the border. The angel kept the guards asleep, grabbed Tuan's hand, and led him out to freedom. Tuan had tried to escape in the past and received torturous punishment, but this time he experienced no fear as he left again.

The angel showed Tuan which road to take and said, "Run!" Tuan ran for his life through the forest in the moonlight. When the sun just started peeking over the horizon, he flagged down a bus.

"I don't have any money, but will you take me?" he asked desperately.

The bus driver said, "Get in!" He took Tuan all the way back to his hometown, where he found a kind stranger who let him make one important call—to his mother.

Tuan's mother was overjoyed to hear her son's voice. Once he was home, Tuan stayed hidden inside for a month, afraid to go outside. He spent that time getting to know his Rescuer, Jesus, through the Bible studies Diu gave him and his mother. They became faithful followers. Three neighbors who witnessed this amazing miracle also started to worship each Sabbath and began studying the Bible in preparation for baptism.

Diu and the other Christians in her country love the Lord so much that they willingly risk their lives to share Him with others. The Lord tells us all to go and spread the gospel (Matthew 28:19, 20), and they take that mandate seriously. Even though the government is communist and they are forbidden to evangelize publicly, they continue to move forward courageously.

Ministries

Adventist Health International

Personal and community health topics have been an integral part of the Adventist message for more than 150 years. The focus on health has gradually evolved into a network of 175 hospitals and 450 clinics operated by the church around the world—half in the United States of America and more than 60 in developing countries. These institutions were largely started in the first half of the twentieth century and have established an impressive reputation in each community they serve.

Over the past forty years, most of these developing countries have gained independence and taken responsibility for their own institutions. This gradual transition has precipitated a decline in external support and expatriate personnel and has often led to a decrease in the quality and effectiveness of these institutions, occasionally resulting in complete closure.

Adventist Health International began more than twenty years ago to help reverse these trends and restore the reputation and impact of each institution. They now assist more than forty hospitals, and the improvement in quality has been demonstrable. With each successful collaboration, the local and national church also gains respect and subsequent growth.

AHI's success has been largely dependent on a growing number of young Adventist professionals and volunteers who, supported by a network of donors, have helped rebuild crumbling infrastructure and replace broken equipment. Even more importantly, AHI has introduced effective governing boards and modern management techniques at each institution. In many countries, Adventist health care is now leading once again in both clinical care and the education of a committed and compassionate workforce.

Website: http://ahiglobal.org
Email: ahi@llu.edu
Phone: 909-558-5610

Amistad International

Amistad International serves impoverished people at the request of communities around the world. Its objective is to share its knowledge and resources as needed and wanted with the understanding that many cultures are fragile and even in danger of disappearing completely. The goal is to be in solidarity with developing communities, helping as they are able but leaving as small a footprint as possible. On average, more than 90 percent of donations go directly to program services. Amistad's work has impacted more than ten countries on three continents, and this is made possible through the generosity of its donor partners and volunteers.

Amistad enables community leaders to teach, develop, and empower the rural poor so that they can participate effectively in their own development. Amistad helps leadership carry out their ideas and vision, knowing their wisdom comes from experience and challenge. Their goal is to help local communities reach economic self-sustenance in culturally inspired and appropriate ways through primary education of children, empowerment of community leadership, water and agriculture training, and trade school programs.

Some of the programs Amistad supports cannot attain economic sustainability because of the nature of the outreach. Among these are elementary schools for impoverished children, orphanages, and a home for HIV-positive children.

They are committed to

- assisting a limited number of worthy projects, run by creative, compassionate people with a high degree of responsibility and accountability;
- stretching the money they receive to help as many as they can using only a minimal amount for foundation expenses;
- maintaining personal relationships with donors and project leaders;
- communicating with their donors frequently about the effect their gifts are having on recipients and workers; and
- letting their donors help them solve problems and work together with them on rewarding projects.

Website: https://www.amistadinternational.org
Email: karen@amistadinternational.org
Phone: 650-328-1737

ASAP Ministries

ASAP, now ASAP Ministries, Inc., has been in operation since 1995 and is a mission organization using Christ's wholistic method to bring hope to the persecuted, poor, unreached, and refugees from the 10/40 window (regions located between 10 and 40 degrees north of the equator). ASAP stands for Advocates for Southeast Asians and the Persecuted. Currently, ASAP Ministries supports more than six hundred church planters, medical missionaries, youth evangelists, and Bible/literacy teachers in the countries of Cambodia, Laos, Thailand, and Myanmar.

ASAP Ministries partners through church planting, medical ministries, literacy programs, schools, evangelism in restricted countries, humanitarian projects such as wells, and refugee resettlement. It is currently supporting more than sixty schools for underprivileged children. Its mission is to train and support Southeast Asian ethnic missionaries and the persecuted to make and multiply disciples using Christ's compassionate methods. ASAP Ministries promotes prayer, disciple-making, church planting, and cross-cultural missions to the world next door.

ASAP Ministries organizes short-term mission trips to Southeast Asia to conduct evangelistic meetings and help with training or with special projects but does not send out missionaries on a long-term basis. Instead, ASAP Ministries supports training and provides stipends for ethnic missionaries who already live in the countries it serves. It uses this method for two reasons: because ethnic missionaries have proven to be extremely effective due to their knowledge of the language and culture, and because it is the most cost-effective method for spreading the gospel. Another unique aspect of ASAP is that donors can specify which project they would like to support, and 100 percent of their donation supports that project. It operates on a faith basis.

Today in Asia thousands are worshipping in faith. Through the Lord's many blessings, ASAP Ministries continues to support the spread of the gospel not only in Cambodia but also in Vietnam, Laos, Thailand, Myanmar, and beyond. To get involved, learn more in the "Take Action" section of the ASAP Ministries website.

Website: http://www.asapministries.org/
Email: office@asapministries.org
Phone: 269-471-3026

Camp Ida-Haven

Camp Ida-Haven is a church camp located on the shores of Payette Lake in McCall, Idaho. McCall is a resort town two hours north of Boise, the capital city of Idaho, and it is surrounded by twenty camps of various affiliations. The Seventh-day Adventist Church purchased eleven acres of ground in 1940 for $1,100. The camp has grown significantly, particularly over the past twenty years, and is currently under the leadership of Douglas and Darla Roe (at camp) and Milford Terrell, its board chair.

In the early 1990s, the camp offered three weeks of youth camps, and sign-up was on the opening day. Present day sign-ups are booked online from late February through early March. In 2018, the entire six weeks of kids' camps sold out in 0.8 seconds (yes, literally). Only 20 to 25 percent of summer and off-season attendees are Seventh-day Adventists and their families. Camp Ida-Haven is purposefully open to guests of all faiths or no faith. It has been awarded "Best of McCall" in the camp category for eleven straight years. The majority of campers come from the Treasure Valley (the greater Boise area), but campers also hail from other US states and many locations around the globe, including China, New Zealand, Alaska, and others.

Camp Ida-Haven's mission is to portray the love of God, regardless of differences. It offers scholarships and, since 2007, has offered a long weekend (Labor Day) to families with special-needs children at no charge. That camp is by invitation only as Ida-Haven is able to make accommodation and is called NeXt Camp, the "next" step.

Website: http://www.idahaven.org
Email: darla@idahaven.org
Phone: 208-634-5922

The Center for Conflict Resolution at La Sierra University

The goal of the Center for Conflict Resolution at La Sierra University is to help resolve actual or potential conflicts and implement peer abuse (bullying) prevention systems that lay the foundation necessary for conflict resolution procedures to function.

While the center's programs and personnel can provide crucial support to reduce the risks posed by threatened or actual litigation, it is also committed to equipping individuals, groups, and organizations to implement peer abuse prevention systems and to deal successfully with conflicts of all kinds. The center's mission is to

- foster interdisciplinary research and programs related to conflict management and peer abuse;
- offer for-credit and noncredit courses and curricula to prepare students to resolve conflicts and prevent peer abuse in business, government, the not-for-profit sector, and their faith communities;
- help people and organizations identify best practices for conflict resolution and peer abuse that will strengthen vital relationships; and
- assist business, governmental, not-for-profit, and religious organizations in resolving conflicts and preventing peer abuse through mediation, negotiation, and facilitation using collaborative, non-adversarial processes and peer abuse prevention training by providing private for-fee casework

as well as pro bono programs, negotiation and advocacy consultation, organizational systems design services, and strategic communication consulting.

La Sierra University is a liberal arts institution affiliated with the Seventh-day Adventist Church, a denomination with a long history of philanthropic service and concern for peace. The center draws gladly on the rich resources of an Adventist tradition that encourages honesty, respect, intelligence, creativity, and openness to peaceful conflict resolution. In particular, the center is responding to the Seventh-day Adventist "Call for Peace" issued by the denomination on April 18, 2002.

Whatever the outcome of the process of resolving a particular conflict, the results for all parties can consistently include satisfaction with the process and an appreciation for training and utilizing individuals who serve as neutrals to help individuals, groups, and organizations address their particular circumstances and needs.

Website: https://lasierra.edu/conflict-resolution/
Email: conflictresolutioncenter@lasierra.edu
Phone: 951-785-2601

Cuba Adventist Theological Seminary

The Seventh-day Adventist Church in Cuba, from its beginnings through 1922, had several elementary schools. In the summer of 1922, the church voted to establish a boarding junior college, Adventist Antillean College, and chose a site in the easternmost province. In 1940, the college moved and became an integrated educational center, including elementary school through junior college. The college served the Adventist youth in all the territory of the Antillean Union: Cuba, Dominican Republic, Haiti, and Puerto Rico.

In 1967, twenty-seven years after its organization and transfer to Santa Clara, the revolutionary government of Cuba expropriated the college as part of its policy of not allowing private schools. For three years after the loss of the campus, the Cuba Union continued to train a very small group of men in the city church of Santa Clara while at the same time seeking government permission to have a seminary limited to the training of pastors. They finally obtained a permit in 1970, but lacking a campus, classes were held in the cramped headquarters of the Cuba Union building near Havana.

Without its own accreditation, in 1987 the seminary provided training as an extension of the Adventist University in Montemorelos, Mexico. In 1995,

Maranatha Volunteers International offered to build a campus for the seminary. The union, convinced of the Lord's guidance, with great sacrifice acquired a property fronting the paved road linking it with Havana.

The college is now accredited as a sixteen-grade institution and has the capacity to board 175 students, though it only has 143 as of 2018. The monthly cost for a boarding student was only forty-six dollars in 2018, but with an average monthly income in Cuba of just twenty dollars, many young women and men who feel called to ministry cannot afford to attend.

Consider helping and send a contribution to the following address:

Email: setac@enet.cu
Fundraising: danchaij@epbfi.com
Phone: 423-505-1264

Enactus

Entrepreneurial—igniting business innovation with integrity and passion.
Action—the experience of social impact that sparks social enterprise.
Us—student, academic, and business leaders collaborating to create a better world.

Enactus is the world's largest experiential learning platform dedicated to creating a better world while developing the next generation of entrepreneurial leaders and social innovators. Enactus has established the largest global business and higher education network in the world. This unique network brings together the knowledge of professional business educators and the expertise of business leaders to focus the potential of university students preparing for leadership roles in business. Its 72,000 students are entrepreneurial, values-driven, social innovators across 1,730 campuses in 36 countries, positively impacting the lives of 1.3 million people each year.

Guided by educators and supported by business leaders, teams of students conduct needs assessments in their communities, identify potential solutions to complex issues, and implement community impact projects. Communities benefit from collaboration and fresh innovation, and students gain valuable experience to advance their personal and professional lives.

As in business, Enactus believes that competition encourages innovation. For Enactus, that means more lives impacted every day. An annual series of regional and national competitions showcases Enactus teams' impacts. Global business leaders judge the entries. National champion teams advance to the prestigious international Enactus World Cup for competition, collaboration, and celebration.

Enactus believes that investing in students who take entrepreneurial action for others creates a better world for everyone. In villages, towns, and cities around the world, Enactus students demonstrate that business has the power to inspire hope, create opportunity where little existed, and ultimately improve lives and strengthen communities. As they succeed at helping others, they develop stronger business and leadership skills as well as a sense of service and responsibility to the community and world around them. In addition, they understand the opportunity for businesses to make a positive economic, social, and environmental impact. Their achievements are the story of Enactus success.

La Sierra University Enactus
Website: http://www.practiceenactus.com
Email: enactus@lasierra.edu
Phone: 951-785-2064

Washington Adventist University Enactus
Website: https://www.wau.edu/Enactus
Email: enactus@wau.edu
Phone: 301-891-4070

Good News TV

Good News TV (GNTV) seeks to connect God's children with our loving Savior, the truths of His Word, and a healthy and active church they can call home. Their mission is to reach metropolitan communities 24/7 with the good news of Christ's love through relevant, inspiring, Christ-centered programs that are unmistakably faithful to the gospel commission and biblical truth. They deliver a balanced variety of the highest quality programs for all ages that inspire vibrant spiritual, mental, physical, and emotional health, leading their viewers to a personal, saving relationship with the loving Creator, and further encouraging continued spiritual growth and Christian service.

GNTV, using Christ-centered programming, introduces its viewers to a better life and future through a personal, saving relationship with the loving Creator.

Its varied programming stresses

- *education* for an optimal life
- *practical applications* for positive change
- *reasoning* together from Scripture
- *importance* of knowing Jesus Christ
- *evidence* through changed lives

- *hope* and *healing* for a better future

Good News TV and GNTV Latino, its English and Spanish TV channels, broadcast messages of hope around the clock. GNTV sincerely appreciates Hope Channel, 3ABN, and other outstanding Adventist media ministries for the excellent messages they provide to air. Each thought-provoking, Christ-centered program introduces viewers to a loving Savior, challenging and encouraging them with truths from Scripture. Good News TV then localizes the channel, inviting viewers to connect with local church families.

GNTV continues to develop relationships with viewers who call for prayer, request literature and DVDs of programs they've watched, or ask for directions to a local Seventh-day Adventist church. Callers report the channel is "such a blessing" and "a lifeline" for them.

Website: http://www.MyGoodNewsTV.com
Email: info@MyGoodNewsTV.com
Phone: 480-264-1116

Helping Hands Caregiver Resource Center

Helping Hands Caregiver Resource Center is a state-licensed adult day care program owned and operated by the Penn Valley Seventh-day Adventist Church. The ministry provides dependent adults a stimulating social environment while giving caregivers a much-needed break with peace of mind. They believe every individual deserves to be treated with dignity and respect, to be encouraged to be as independent as possible, and to be empowered to form peer relationships and engage in social events as the person is able.

While at Helping Hands, participants experience improved quality of daily living through socialization and peer friendships, quality entertainment, exercise, and other purposeful activities. Helping Hands emphasizes physical activities and cognitive stimulation to help improve independence and alertness, stimulate memory and awareness, and improve self-worth and interactions with others. Participants receive a drink and a breakfast snack as well as a full lunch with dessert daily. A registered nurse is always present to assist with medications, and all staff members are trained to assist with mobility and personal hygiene.

During the program day, participants enjoy a variety of participant-driven activities. Local artists provide music each month, which often brings moments of clarity to those with dementia. Dancing gets many up and moving while professionally trained staff provide support for those who are at risk of a fall. Sing-alongs and pet visits are participant favorites. The big-screen projection system allows everyone to enjoy "going to the movies" each month, and everyone seems to love the arts and crafts they can make to take home and share with loved ones. Every participant is valued and able to express his or her desires regarding activities. Dignity is the rule, where being respected regardless of disability or infirmity means everyone's needs are met competently and with compassion.

Website: http://www.nchelpinghands.org
Phone: 530-432-2540

Holbrook Indian School

Holbrook Indian School (HIS) was established in 1946 and is a first- through twelfth-grade Christian boarding school operated by the Pacific Union of the Seventh-day Adventist Church. When it opened, there were no desks, and the children had to sit on rugs and sheepskins to recite their lessons. As the second school year was coming to an end, the first Adventist Navajo church in Arizona was organized at the school and boasted seventeen members.

The campus is located on 214 acres in Holbrook, Arizona, near the border of the Navajo Nation. Most of the students are Navajo (Diné). Youth from the Apache, Havasupai, Pima, Lakota, Crow, Blackfoot, Hopi, Hualapai, Sioux, Yavapai, and Algonquin tribes have also attended Holbrook throughout the years. HIS also operates Chinle Adventist Elementary School, a day school comprising grades 1–8 located in Chinle, Arizona, within the borders of the Navajo Nation.

HIS provides a safe, nurturing environment where students can discover their strengths as well as identify and overcome their weaknesses. They obtain the resources, skills, and tools they need to face the challenges of the conflicting worlds (Native reservations versus Western society and Native traditions versus Christianity) in which they live. Youth come to HIS with unimaginable challenges. Post-traumatic stress disorder (PTSD), substance abuse, and trust and abandonment issues seem to be the norm. HIS helps students reclaim their identity and develop their intellect in a Christian-values-based curriculum. Students learn academic discipline, are encouraged to be stewards of their heritage, and demonstrate servant leadership in their communities.

Former students have become nurses, lawyers, business owners, community leaders, pastors, human services agents, teachers, members of the US armed forces, school administrators, Gates Millennial Scholars, judges, and even a chief mechanic for the US Navy Blue Angels Flight Demonstration Squadron. But more than that, Holbrook's alumni go on to live lives built on the knowledge that they are deeply loved by their Creator.

Website: http://HolbrookIndianSchool.org
Email: development@hissda.org
Phone: 928-524-6845

Hope Channel

Hope Channel is a Christian television network with forty-six channels around the world broadcasting in fifty-seven languages. Its mission is to share God's good news for a better life today and for eternity. The programs focus on faith, health, relationships, and community. Good spiritual and educational content is important, not only because of Hope Channel's standards, but also because of the impact it has on the lives of thousands of viewers. Knowing that people around the world are coming to Christ through Hope Channel, the network is committed to acquiring and airing powerful, life-changing programs.

Programs on each channel are contextualized for local culture and are broadcast in many languages, including Spanish, Portuguese, German, Romanian, Mandarin, Russian, Tamil, Hindi, Ukrainian, Arabic, Farsi, and Telugu. There are many ways to watch Hope Channel.

Supporting the belief that true inner peace and contentment are found only in Jesus Christ, Hope Channel's programs communicate the following core biblical beliefs:

- God is love, and He has revealed Himself in His Son, Jesus Christ (1 John 4:16; John 14:9).
- Jesus is the divine Son of God; not a created being, but the eternal God (John 1:1).
- Jesus came to this earth to live a perfect life and give His life on the cross to redeem us from our sin (Romans 5:6–10).
- When Jesus comes into our lives, He makes us new creatures (2 Corinthians 5:17; Hebrews 8:10; John 14:15).
- Bible prophecy reveals that the end of this world is imminent and that Jesus will return soon (Revelation 22:12).
- We are commissioned to share Jesus with others and be prepared for Jesus' soon return (Revelation 22:17).

Website: https://www.hopetv.org/
Email: info@hopetv.org
Phone: 888-446-7388

International Children's Care

Christian laypeople organized International Children's Care (ICC) in 1978. In the beginning, its purpose was to meet a need in Guatemala after a devastating earthquake left many children homeless, but it has since expanded to other areas of need in the world. From the beginning, ICC resolved that it would not create a typical orphanage, but rather a unique program designed to consider the mental, emotional, spiritual, and physical needs of the child. In other words, they would provide not simply food and a roof, but homes and families in an atmosphere that would bring love and security to the children.

Therefore, ICC started the cottage group-home plan. Instead of living in large groups in one building, the children live in individual homes on small acreages. National couples serve as parents to groups of ten to twelve children per home, forming a family. This arrangement avoids an institutional-style setting. The long-term results are much more positive, enabling children to learn basic skills and relate normally to life.

Education is an important part of the program. ICC operates elementary schools on its grounds, adapting the school program to the needs of the children. It provides education through high school and even on to college or university when the young person shows interest and ability.

The farm is an integral part of the program. It provides work opportunities for the older children, and it helps provide food and lessens the need for outside help. Also, the children learn manual skills, thus preparing them to face life on their own someday.

Each home operates on Christian principles, with morning and evening worship geared to the interest of small children. In this atmosphere, the children learn to be true Christians, making the Bible the foundation of their faith.

Website: http://www.forhiskids.org
Email: info@forhiskids.org
Phone: 360-573-0429

La Sierra University Center for Near Eastern Archaeology

The Center for Near Eastern Archaeology at La Sierra University engages and collaborates with local and global communities to foster interest in and develop an appreciation for the ancient cultures of the Near East. Accordingly, the center responsibly conserves and displays its artifacts from the Near East in a manner mutually beneficial for both the communities from which the artifacts came and the community in which they now reside.

As part of an academic institution, it provides educational resources and research opportunities for students, scholars, and the public. By promoting awareness of the past, especially the biblical past, the center constructs a better future for religious and secular communities alike.

The center, together with other universities, sponsors the Madaba Plains Project, with excavations at Tall Hisban, Tall al-ʿUmayri (primary sponsor), and Tall Jalul. The sites are located to the east of the Jordan River in the fertile highlands overlooking the Dead Sea. The region, home to various people groups for millennia, was rich in agricultural capacity. Major settlements occupied ʿUmayri and Jalul in the Bronze Age (3300–1200 B.C.), including a massive defense system at ʿUmayri in 1600 B.C. (the time of the patriarchs and matriarchs), which reflects the need to protect people and property. An ʿUmayri temple from 1300 B.C. (the time of Moses) signals the importance of religion to the ancients. The Iron Age (1200–500 B.C., the time of the judges and kings), extremely well represented at all three sites by architecture and other material cultural remains, saw tribal groups settling down and witnessed the rise of small kingdoms, known in the Bible as Ammonites and Moabites. Hisban revealed remains from later periods, including temples and reservoirs from Greek and Roman times (the fourth century B.C. through third century A.D.); mosaic floors and church architecture from the Byzantine period of the sixth and seventh centuries; rich building remains from the Middle Islamic period, especially Mamluk times in the twelfth and thirteenth centuries A.D.; and structures and artifacts from the Late Islamic periods.

Website: https://www.lasierra.edu/archaeology
Email: archaeology@lasierra.edu
Phone: 951-785-2632

Mamawi Atosketan Native School

Canada's Mamawi Atosketan Native School, a First Nations school operated by the relatively small Alberta Conference, is unique in North America: a church-run First Nations school of more than two hundred students is almost unheard of in post-residential-school Canada. Established in 2003 to serve the four bands of the Maskwacis Cree Nation between Wetaskiwin and Ponoka, Alberta, Mamawi Atosketan Native School (MANS) is a successful, accredited, and privately funded K–12 school. It is a violence-free learning community that integrates proven practices of physical, mental, spiritual, and social well-being into each day in a distinctly Cree environment.

Mamawi Atosketan—which means "working together" in Cree—has become a living reality for school families. Mutual respect coupled with innovative thinking and an attitude of partnership has produced a new generation of parents and students engaged in the day-to-day process of education. Parents see the changes in the lives of their children: they see learners who feel safe, who grow in confidence, and who are eager to get to school and enthusiastic about what happens there.

The dynamic has changed. The conversations about education are different: graduating from high school and university is no longer an unreachable dream, but an attainable goal.

In 2011, based on student and parent requests, MANS began adding high school classes, one grade at a time. Until then, their students had to leave MANS for another school at the very moment they were primed for high school success. As a result, too many of their students fell through the cracks and dropped out of their next school—becoming part of Canada's First Nations education tragedy.

To succeed in any culture, the Cree youth of Maskwacis need a complete high school experience—one that not only teaches Alberta university-track and vocational courses but also allows students to consider new options and outcomes and to handle responsibility in a supportive environment. MANS is dedicated to providing an excellent academic and vocational program that responds to each student's cultural and academic needs within a safe and caring rural environment where the character and skills necessary for leadership can be cultivated and service to others becomes a way of life.

Website: http://www.mans1.ca
Email: TheBridge@mans1.ca
Phone: 403-342-5044 ext. 233

Pine Springs Ranch

Pine Springs Ranch Christian Youth Camp and Retreat Center is owned and operated by the Southeastern California Conference of Seventh-day Adventists. The camp is located on 481 acres near Mountain Center, California, in the beautiful San Jacinto Mountains. The site was purchased in 1961, replacing a 16-acre facility in nearby Idyllwild. Originally built to be a ranch-style summer camp, it has grown into one of the largest and most modern camps and retreat centers of its kind on the West Coast.

Pine Springs Ranch has several buildings on-site providing a variety of retreat meeting options. The main lodge contains two floors with seventy-nine hotellike rooms. North Village and South Village each have ten cabins, which house summer campers and retreat visitors. Those wanting a rustic experience can sleep in teepees or wagons. There are four outdoor meeting areas: Church Bowl, Campfire Bowl, the Fort, and Teepees. The facility features a pool, a go-cart track, an archery range, a horseshoe pit, basketball courts, a high and low ropes challenge course, and more.

Pine Springs Ranch Retreat Center provides an opportunity for those wanting to get away and encounter God through nature. Many people have experienced life-changing moments at Pine Springs Ranch. It is truly a place of transformation.

The Christian Youth Camp's mission is "Calling campers to Christ." The goal is for kids to have a safe, positive Christian experience in the great outdoors. Campers can practice decision-making skills and experience a taste of independence. At Pine Springs Ranch they meet positive Christian role models—young adults who are setting a good example every day. They can take a break from social media and make new friends, try new things, and experience success in a safe place.

Website: https://www.psr.camp/ and https://www.pinespringsranch.org/
Email: PSRCamp@seccsda.org
Phone: 951-509-2267

Project Patch

Tom and Bonnie Sanford started Project Patch with the dream of helping struggling youth. They knew that troubled teens are hurting teens, and they longed to give them safety and a new chance at life.

Project Patch began in 1984 as a referral and foster placement program. As the need to place youth escalated and it became increasingly difficult to find enough foster homes, the Patch Board of Trustees began to pray for a place to house young people.

In 1989, a gift of 116 acres in southern Idaho that included riverfront acreage, along with the purchase of an adjacent 53 acres, provided the possibility of fulfilling this dream of a place for hurting teens. Many miracles, many volunteers, and many generous donors later, workers finished construction on residence halls and the main lodge with beautiful views of the river.

Project Patch Youth Program is nationally recognized for its highly effective therapeutic and spiritual care of hurting teens. The program is Joint Commission-accredited, licensed by the state of Idaho, and operates an AdvancED accredited school on their campus. Since 1993, more than one thousand teenagers have been physically, emotionally, and spiritually renewed at the Project Patch youth programs. Boise State University and Walla Walla University studies show

Project Patch is very effective in helping teens and families.

Project Patch is passionately committed to building thriving families, restoring hope to teens, and empowering supportive communities. The mission to help teens now includes a program for the entire family designed to help them pull together. The Project Patch Family Experience is a retreat that uses teaching, fun activities, discussions, and recreation to help families.

Project Patch also offers seminars on parenting topics for churches, schools, and communities across the United States. Common topics include technology addiction and motivating unmotivated teens.

Website: https://www.projectpatch.org
Email: info@projectpatch.org
Phone: 360-690-8495

Scheer Memorial Adventist Hospital

In the late 1950s when Nepal opened its doors to the outside world, Dr. Stanley and Raylene Sturges and their children were the first Seventh-day Adventist medical missionaries to Nepal. They asked King Mahendra where they could be most useful, and he sent them to the village of Banepa, east of the nation's capital, Kathmandu.

The Sturgeses began with just a small, one-room clinic, caring for the immediate and urgent medical needs of the community. By 1960, they had expanded into a twenty-bed hospital. At that time, Scheer Memorial Hospital was the only hospital serving the half-million people in the region.

Since those modest early years, Scheer Memorial Adventist Hospital has evolved into a three-story, 150-bed facility that provides a full range of outpatient and inpatient services. Professional medical teams from America, Netherlands, Australia, and Japan run free annual health camps at Scheer providing surgical repairs for burn victims, uterine prolapse patients, and cleft lip or cleft palate patients.

Nepal is one of the poorest nations in the world; one-third of Nepal's population lives below the poverty line. In Banepa, Nepal, where Scheer is located, many in the region can't afford the cost of a health-care consultation, which often amounts to less than forty cents in US dollars. Scheer doesn't turn anyone away for inability to pay. People come from miles around, traveling on foot from rural villages with no roads, electricity, or adequate health care. Some even come carrying sick family members on their backs because they know they will be welcome, regardless of finances.

Scheer Memorial Adventist Hospital is more than just a hospital. It is a community support system and a safe haven for everyone. Beyond serving the region's medical needs, they also provide education for elementary school children and welcome many volunteers from around the world who want to make a difference in Nepal.

Website: https://www.scheermemhosp.org/
Email: scheerhospital@gmail.com
International: +977-1-166-1111 or 1112
Nepal: 01-166-1111 or 1112

Thunderbird Adventist Academy

Thunderbird Adventist Academy is an oasis of citrus and palm trees located in the middle of Scottsdale, Arizona. Originally named Arizona Academy and founded in 1920, the school changed its name and moved to its present location after buying Thunderbird Field II, a World War II pilot training facility. In the intervening years, the campus changed, buildings and classrooms were replaced, and the city of Scottsdale grew up around the campus. But in its small corner of verdant tranquility, Thunderbird Academy holds true to its founding aim of developing the spiritual, mental, and physical faculties of its students.

The school's goal is for each of its students to EXCEL: to *experience* Jesus, to *communicate* clearly and think critically, to *embrace* service and citizenship, and to *live* healthfully in body and mind. They promote the development of habits that will last a lifetime by helping students grow spiritually, excel academically, mature socially, and practice positive health habits.

Thunderbird goes beyond traditional course offerings. In addition to standard high school classes, it provides honors courses and college credit options in several subject areas. Further, Thunderbird's private pilot and certified nursing assistant programs provide pathways for individuals interested in careers in aviation or the health-care industry. Thunderbird is one of a handful of high schools in the United States where students can take classes toward their private pilot certificate. Adventist World Aviation partners with the school to give students instruction for both the ground and flight portions of their training. The certified nursing assistant (CNA) program allows students to take their Arizona State Boards and graduate as CNAs, which provides a jump-start for a variety of careers in the healthcare industry.

Website: https://www.thunderbirdacademy.org
Email: info@thunderbirdacademy.org
Phone: 480-948-3300

The Unforgettables Foundation

Timothy Evans is an ordained Seventh-day Adventist pastor of thirty years who has ministered in churches at and around Andrews University in Berrien Springs, Michigan; Kettering University in Flint, Michigan; Takoma Park, Maryland; and Loma Linda, California, and is a founding chaplain of Loma Linda University Children's Hospital. In 1999 he founded The Unforgettables Foundation, a 501(c)(3) nonprofit organization. Through a decade of clinical ministry to children and their families, Evans assisted many families through crisis following the death of a child. He witnessed firsthand the crushing financial burdens families with limited resources experienced when faced with burying their child.

Assisted by Inland Empire educators, medical professionals, social workers, CPAs (certified public accountants), attorneys, bankers, morticians, and others, Evans created The Unforgettables Foundation. Paramount among aspects of the foundation's mission is to assist low-income families in providing a dignified, appropriate burial for their children who have passed away.

The mission of The Unforgettables Foundation is to

- enable low-income families to give their children a dignified burial;
- empower communities to memorialize children who have died;
- educate parents and children's caregivers to confront, control, and conquer the primary risks to a child's health and wholeness; and
- encourage communities to recognize the financial trauma that is often associated with the death of a child.

The Unforgettables Foundation provides financial assistance to families with limited resources to help offset the costs of final arrangements. Requests for aid come from hospitals, social service agencies, and families themselves. Since its creation, the foundation has assisted more than five thousand families in more than eighty cities in Southern California.

Many childhood deaths are preventable with the proper education to recognize the signs, symptoms, and vulnerabilities that children face in their daily lives. The Unforgettables Foundation also presents information, skills, and knowledge to prepare communities and those who work with children to recognize the deadly risks that children face and to be equipped to help prevent the deaths of children associated with these risks.

Website: http://www.unforgettables.org
Email: tevans@theunforgettables.com
Phone: 909-335-1600

Water for Life International

Water for Life International (WFL) is a Spokane, Washington–based, non-profit charity dedicated to bringing the blessings of safe drinking water and the gospel to remote villages in northeast Guatemala. The charity started in 2004 as an endeavor of volunteers working to solve a contaminated drinking water problem at a school and orphanage in Guatemala. With the blessing of God, it has grown into a well-equipped ministry drilling water wells in remote villages. With 113 wells in operation, WFL provides water for about thirty thousand people every day. In addition, it maintains the wells.

Water for Life has a loyal group of volunteers who come from across the country to use their skills to benefit people. They use WFL equipment and drill in villages where people have no source of safe drinking water. The World Health Organization points to waterborne illness as the greatest killer of children in the world. Water for Life is on the front lines of the battle to save children. One village leader remarked to a volunteer who came to check on the well, "This is the first year that no child has died in our village."

Drilling water wells is a natural platform for spreading the gospel. WFL's workers respect the Sabbath, and villagers learn from WFL Bible teachers and from the thousands of Bible study guides and Spanish Bibles WFL distributes each year. Water for Life provides vehicles, housing, and support for church and conference groups who go to Guatemala on mission projects. It has assisted in the construction of fourteen Seventh-day Adventist churches in the area. Drilling wells that provide pure water to bring health and sharing Bible truths and the gospel of Jesus is the real work of Water for Life.

Website: https://www.h2oforlife.org
Email: info.waterforlife@gmail.com
Phone: 208-907-0010

Your Story Hour

Your Story Hour, a worldwide, nondenominational children's radio ministry, began when Stanley Hill and Jay Clymer formed a Saturday afternoon story hour group with other adults and college young people. They told stories, bringing them to life for their audience of neighborhood children. The story hour was an immediate success and eventually transitioned to radio. Almost from the beginning, Your Story Hour offered a Bible school program featuring *Adventures in the Holy Bible* lessons. It later added a magazine, *Clubhouse*. Both continue to be an integral part of the ministry's outreach.

In 1985 Your Story Hour launched a Spanish version of the radio program, *Tu Historia Preferida*. The Spanish program hosts' voices became as recognizable in Central and South America, Mexico, the Caribbean, and Spain as their English counterparts are. *Tu Historia Preferida* also launched Bible clubs that reached thousands of children throughout the Latin world.

Your Story Hour expanded again in 1992 with a Russian-language program. *Chas Tvoego Rasskaza* originally aired on the government radio station during the last months of the Soviet Union. *Chas Tvoego Rasskaza* also offered a Bible study booklet based on the English *Adventures* course, which was widely distributed throughout Russia.

Through the years, Your Story Hour has created hundreds of fully dramatized programs that are written to encourage children through the retelling of inspirational and educational events and featuring the people who faced enormous adversities but were able to achieve great things in life. They highlight the importance of perseverance, honesty, kindness, trusting in God, obedience, and a host of other character-building traits.

Your Story Hour's listenership has expanded through the years, with approximately four thousand radio stations currently airing the programs. It's hard to imagine that what started out as a small afternoon storytime turned into a worldwide ministry reaching millions of children over the years.

Website: https://www.yourstoryhour.org
Email: contact@yourstoryhour.org
Phone: 800-987-7879

Youth and Family Life Education Institute

Youth and Family Life Education Institute helps communities provide services and resources to underserved, at-risk youth and families through education, cultural outreach, and hands-on, frontline help.

The ministry's main office is located in Montgomery, Alabama, and the institute is a 501(c)(3) charity. From helping families through death and disasters to providing computer education for seniors to promoting youth and women's initiatives, the ministry has served Montgomery's inner city and surrounding areas since 2000.

One of the ministry's most visible efforts focuses on the empowerment of women and girls through school-based classes and abuse awareness and prevention campaigns. Empowerment opportunities for girls in grades six to twelve exist through the "Making of a Lady" program. One of the program's components includes Girl Life classes taught at selected schools during the school day.

In these classes, the foundations of empowerment—character, leadership, academics, service, and sisterhood—are central as students work on self-esteem and conflict resolution issues. Additionally, the program helps supply school needs and other necessities. Lastly, program participants receive abuse education and opportunities to give back to their communities.

Along with Making of a Lady, other programs, past and present, include the Community Technology Assistance Program, providing computers and youth and senior computer classes; the Community Literacy Project, a reading project that involves middle and elementary students throughout the school system; and Help the Women (abuse awareness and prevention campaigns).

The institute's founder and CEO Sandra Hawkins, MEd, MAT, a retired public-school educator, and her group of volunteers are committed to the mission of helping underserved youth and families now and into the future.

Email: sandrahawkins70@gmail.com
Phone: 334-279-7850
Youth and Family Life Education Institute
P.O. Box 241325
Montgomery, Alabama 36117

Zoz Amba Foundation

Adu Worku founded the Zoz Amba Foundation to provide education and resources to help the people of his native Ethiopia. Zoz Amba is a steep-sided and flat-topped mountain near his home village in northwest Ethiopia, and it was chosen as a metaphor of life in rural Ethiopia. Worku knew from experience that peasant life was like that mountain—steep!

Zoz Amba's goal in doing community projects is to help villagers climb the mountain of life for the better view at the top, just like the panoramic view afforded by Zoz Amba's flat top. They use the acronym OATS, for ownership, accountability, transparency, and sustainability, when designing, evaluating, and implementing any of their projects. In laying the groundwork further, they adopted another acronym, ALPS—affordable, local, practical, safe—words closely tied to ownership and sustainability. They strongly believed that following their guiding principles would open doors, and it has.

Zoz Amba strives to collaborate with community leaders, faith groups, local government agencies, and NGOs to support sustainable development in rural Ethiopia, with special emphasis on issues affecting women and girls. Their vision is to empower women and girls in rural Ethiopia by eradicating genital cutting, early marriage, and illiteracy and by providing access to clean water, flour mills, and training on basic health and hygiene.

All the projects they offer improve the quality of life for women and girls, and education is key. An African proverb states, "If you educate a man you educate an individual, but if you educate a woman you educate a family (nation)."

Website: http://www.zozamba.org
Email: info@zozamba.org